CHRISTMAS AROUND THE VILLAGE GREEN

Derbyshire, 1940s: Christmas is different for little Dot May Dunn and her fellow villagers these days. The paper garlands are red, white and blue, though Father Christmas still comes, carols are sung, and families are relieved to be together. As the seasons change and war still rages, Dot must adjust to holidays, village fetes and school life under its shadow. She understands very little of the terrible events in the adult world; but as the village comes face to face with their effects, the real impact bears heavily on this close-knit mining community.

CHRISTMAS AROUND THE VILLAGE GREEN

In a WWII rural village, family
means the world at Christmas

DOT MAY DUNN

ISIS
LARGE
PRINT

First published in Great Britain 2015
by
Orion
an imprint of the Orion Publishing Group Ltd.

First Isis Edition
published 2016
by arrangement with
Orion Publishing Group Ltd.
An Hachette UK Company

A catalogue record for this book is available
from the British Library.

ISBN 978–1–78541–259–2 (hb)
ISBN 978–1–78541–265–3 (pb)

Published by
F. A. Thorpe (Publishing)
Anstey, Leicestershire

Set by Words & Graphics Ltd.
Anstey, Leicestershire
Printed and bound in Great Britain by
T. J. International Ltd., Padstow, Cornwall

This book is printed on acid-free paper

For my brother Trev, Jack in the story, who
unfortunately died before this book was finished.

Acknowledgements

I would like to thank Amanda Harris, Orion Publisher, and Gillian Stern, my brilliant editor, who made it possible for me to find this book in a chaos of stories. Also to my brothers, Trev and Bill, who helped to remind me of those far-off days.

A note to the reader: while this book is about true events, which are in time and of essence, I would like to remind you that all of it has been filtered through 75 years of memory — think on!

Contents

Contents

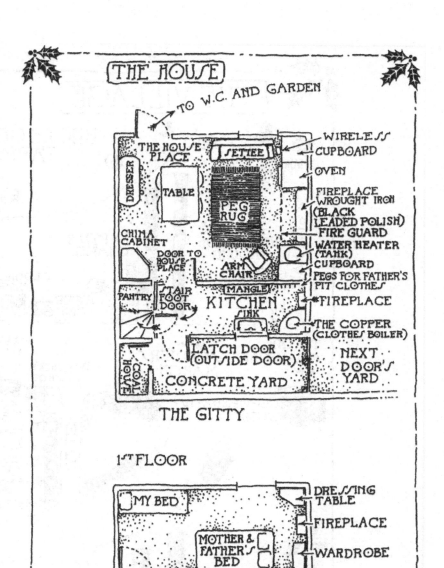

THE HOUSE

TO W.C. AND GARDEN

WIRELESS
CUPBOARD

THE HOUSE PLACE

SETTEE

OVEN

FIREPLACE WROUGHT IRON (BLACK LEADED POLISH)

DRESSER

TABLE

PEG RUG

FIRE GUARD

WATER HEATER (TANK) CUPBOARD

CHINA CABINET

PEGS FOR FATHER'S PIT CLOTHES

DOOR TO HOUSE PLACE

ARM CHAIR

*FIREPLACE

PANTRY

STAIR FOOT DOOR

MANGLE

KITCHEN SINK

THE COPPER (CLOTHES BOILER)

COAL HOUSE

LATCH DOOR (OUTSIDE DOOR)

NEXT DOOR'S YARD

CONCRETE YARD

THE GITTY

1st FLOOR

MY BED

DRESSING TABLE

FIREPLACE

MOTHER & FATHER'S BED

WARDROBE

LANDING

BED

STORAGE CUPBOARD

BOYS' BEDROOM

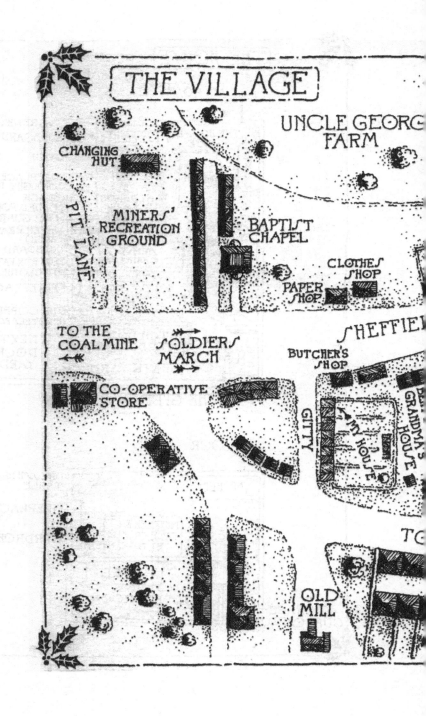

THE VILLAGE

UNCLE GEORGE FARM

CHANGING HUT

PIT LANE

MINERS' RECREATION GROUND

BAPTIST CHAPEL

CLOTHES SHOP

PAPER SHOP

TO THE COAL MINE

SOLDIERS MARCH

SHEFFIELD

BUTCHER'S SHOP

GITTY

MY HOUSE

GRANDMA'S HOUSE

CO-OPERATIVE STORE

OLD MILL

TO

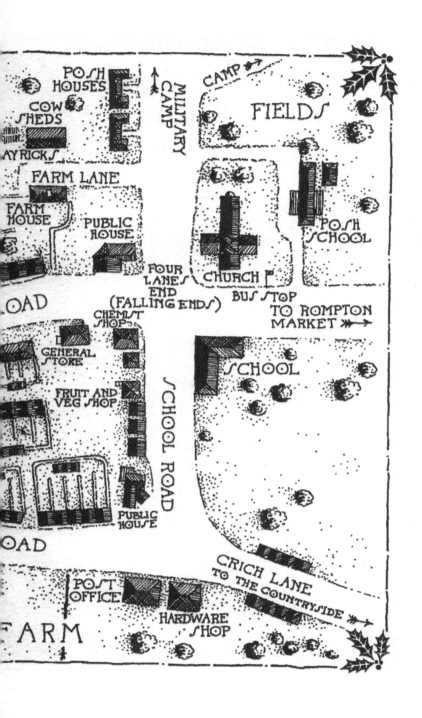

POSH
HOUSES

COW
SHEDS

AYRICKS

FARM LANE

FARM
HOUSE

PUBLIC
HOUSE

MILITARY CAMP

CAMP

FIELDS

FOUR
LANES
END
(FALLING ENDS)

CHURCH

POSH
SCHOOL

BUS STOP
TO ROMPTON
MARKET

OAD

CHEMIST
SHOP

GENERAL
STORE

FRUIT AND
VEG SHOP

SCHOOL ROAD

SCHOOL

PUBLIC
HOUSE

OAD

CRICH LANE
TO THE COUNTRYSIDE

POST
OFFICE

HARDWARE
SHOP

FARM

CHAPTER
ONE

Carol singing

December 1940

I am five and a half years old. It's the Christmas holidays and I'm waiting. Waiting for the war to be over. Everyone said the war would be over by last Christmas, but it's still going and when I asked Father if it would be over this Christmas, in two days' time, he shook his head and looked sad.

I'm also waiting for Christmas. Yesterday we decorated the pine branch that Father cut down from a tree in the village, put up the holly and finished making the paper garlands — painting them red, white and blue this year for the men fighting in the war — and I helped Mother with the baking. And now I sit here, waiting, waiting, waiting. At least the wireless is on and I can hear carols. I listen out for the ones I will be singing with the Chapel choir tonight, so I can run through the words in my head. I never get "In the Bleak Midwinter" right.

A snowflake drifts past. I press my face to the glass and peer through the foggy window as it disappears. I look for the snow fairies on a drop of water and as it sets off from the top of the window, I catch it with my finger.

"*Dorothy!* Will you keep your sticky fingers off those windows? Don't you think I've got enough to do getting ready for Christmas."

My mother's angry voice startles me. The wooden settee rocks backwards. I think: "*And get down from that settee.*"

"And get down from that settee."

I turn and face my mother. Her blue-grey eyes are flashing dangerously. She is hot and red-faced and as she pushes the bits of escaped hair under the band around her head, she glares at me.

I can smell just-baked cake and a pie. As I jump down, I can see the cake as it sits cooling on a wire tray. The pie — Father's Special Christmas Veal Pie — is still in the oven, but in my mind I can see its brown top and hear the sizzling meat stewing in its juices.

"Take the mixing bowl into the kitchen, Dorothy, and don't drop it. I'll never be able to buy a new one with this war on. Can't buy food, now we are on the ration, never mind pots to put it in. At least we got more tea and sugar for Christmas. Though I still get confused about what colour ration book matches what food."

The war has made things all different. When we go shopping now we have to take yellow, green and blue books with coupons in them. And when we go outside we have to carry our Mickey Mouse masks in case there is a gas attack in the air. At school we have gas drills where we practise pulling them out of the cardboard

2

boxes and onto our faces as quickly as possible. We have to get them off as fast as possible too, before everyone blows down the tube and makes rude noises. I hate the rubbery smell and my face feeling all squished up. Our teacher, Miss Mallory, makes us say where we live. She says that in this war children are being separated from their families so we must remember where we live, what our father's name is and who is in our family. As I head to the sink I remember the words that I had said to the teacher this morning. "My name is Dot, I'm five and a lot, my father Joe, he mines the coal. I have two brothers, Jack and Bob, my mum's called Nellie, we're all called Compton and we live near Rompton." I say this to myself when I am out, in case a German comes down from the sky and takes me.

The war has made Mother worry and the worry has made her cough. She is always working in the house and she gets very tired. Sometimes, when the weather is cold, she can't get to sleep for the coughing. I sleep in a little bed in the corner of Mother and Father's bedroom and sometimes Father lights a fire in the small fireplace in our bedroom so she is warm. Some mornings when she gets up she looks poorly, with rings around her eyes and a white face. Then I think I shouldn't go to school, that I should stay behind and help her, but she says I am better off going to learn my lessons. There is a lot to learn "out there", she always says, "and you need to learn more than I ever did, especially to get on round here". Mother isn't from round here, she grew up in London and once told me,

3

when she had had a fight with Aunt Lily, that she wished she'd never left "civilisation".

The green velvety curtain, which hangs down between our kitchen and the houseplace, blows outward. It's Jack, my big brother, coming back from school. Jack is now eight years old and he goes to the big boys' school and has to stay later than me.

Mother is on guard, arms around her new cake.

"Close that door before you ruin this cake."

Jack slides himself through the curtain. He is tall and slim and as he peels his hat off, his normally sticky-out hair is wet against his face.

"What?" he asks, his breathing short after the change of air from iced to warm. "It's freezing out there."

His face is shiny and his coat looks snow-wet. I'm sure he's been snowballing on the way home, even though he's not allowed.

"I'll give you what if you've made this cake go flat."

Taking no notice of Mother's threats, my brother, who would eat cake all day if he could, peers through her arms.

"Is it our Christmas cake?"

"No, not really." Mother sighs. "I couldn't get the currants or the sultanas. The woman at the shop in Rompton said she had to ration them, though who she rationed them to I don't know. She didn't give me any. I've put what fruit I did get in the pudding."

She nods towards the double pan that simmers on the side of the fire, steam rising.

"This war is getting worse, can't get anything to cook with," she says sadly.

4

We stirred the pudding mixture yesterday throughout the day, taking turns to hold the spoon. We added some of Father's stout and five silver threepenny pieces and now it's only two days until we see who finds the coins. I always eat my Christmas pudding slowly because if you swallow the money it's a disaster. Jack told me quite vividly what happened when he swallowed a coin.

Now we all stand and look at the puddings as they gently boil in the large pan, each basin wrapped and tied in a piece of old white pillowcase. Mother leans across the fireguard and slides the big pan a little further onto the boiler top and away from the hot fire.

"Don't want these to spoil. I've put all the fruit I could get into them. I want *something* to taste like it used to before this war came."

"Do you think we'll still be carol singing in this snow?" Jack asks as he peels off his coat and scarf and throws them over the corduroy cushions on Father's chair. I wonder how he thinks he will get away with that. Every day when Father returns from work he wheels his bicycle through the kitchen door, leans it on the wall by the stair-foot door, takes off his pit boots, puts them under the mangle in the cold dark kitchen, hangs his dusty coat and hat on the pegs, slips on his felt slippers, walks through the curtain and falls into his armchair, over which Mother has put an old grey blanket to stop the coal getting everything dirtier. As he sinks into his chair he reaches over to the mantelpiece, takes down his pipe and begins the job of lighting it. Nothing must get in the way of this ritual. Mother will

5

have something to say about Jack's coat soon enough. I count to three in my head.

"Hey, you!" she shouts. "Hang that coat up, never mind decorating your father's chair."

Her sharp words wake up Bob, my baby brother. He has been asleep in his pram and now his blue eyes are blinking open.

"And now you've got Bob up," snaps Mother. "Dot, go and stop him climbing out of the pram while I get this sago pudding out of the oven."

Bob throws his short, fat arms around me and puts his hands in my hair. "Dodo, Dodo," he murmurs. He's all soft and warm. I lift him out — he's a bit heavy now he's three — and set him down. He toddles on his feet, unsteady as his legs start working.

I open the table drawer and lift out the tablecloth. It will be teatime now Jack is back and Bob is up.

"And don't put the cloth on. I've got some pastry to roll in a minute," Mother calls as she carries Bob off into the kitchen.

We listen as he squeals. Mother always washes his face under the cold tap when he wakes up. When he returns his face is bright red and he's wearing clean trousers and socks; she must have stood him in the sink and washed his bottom. I shudder. I remember that feeling of shock when you wake up from a warm sleep and get put under the cold tap.

"Your turn," she says, looking at Jack and me.

In the kitchen the white pail stands under the sink, bleach water in its bottom. The block of carbolic soap is ready for us. I complete the job with care. I don't want

Mother coming to my aid or I will get several parts of myself washed in the cold water. Anyway, I need to talk to Jack.

"All good for later?" I ask. "Who's in?"

I've been waiting for tonight too. First, Jack and I are going around the village, carol singing with the Chapel choir, and afterwards we are going to break off and go singing with Jack's friends — who are now mine too — to earn ourselves a penny or two. Albert, who we call Bert, and his twin brother Arthur are our best friends because our mother is friends with their mother. They might be twins but they are very different from each other. Arthur is clever and quiet and looks out for his brother, who is tubby and has a squint so it looks as if his eyes are half-shut all the time. Bert isn't as sharp and fast as everyone else, though he doesn't stop talking, and he always waits for me when things go too quickly. He is very, very kind and I love him inside my heart. Unlike Harry, who is not very nice to me. He doesn't think girls should be in the gang and he makes things as difficult as he can for me.

Last year, I was so cold during the Chapel choir carols that Aunt Flo had to take me home early. I never heard the end of it from Harry, who called me a "no-good girl sissy". George, his younger brother, who is now in the Juniors, thinks he knows everything and can't stop telling us about the war; he's always on the lookout for Germans. Mike is the best at singing and we need him along tonight if we are to make any money. Besides, his mother thinks he will die of starvation if he doesn't have food in his pockets, so he

7

always has something to share. When Mike sings it makes me go all shivery and I feel sad thinking of his father, who died when he was down the mine.

As we scrub our hands, Jack and I hatch our plans for later, the running water drowning out our words so Mother can't hear.

"Who's coming?" I ask.

"Mike, Harry and George, for definite. Bert and Arthur might come after Chapel, but Bert had a sore throat today, so I don't know."

"I don't think that will stop him looking for money." Bert likes to earn a penny or two.

When we go back into the houseplace, Mother is looking out of the window. The snow has stopped and the sky looks a little lighter. A large brown bowl sits in the middle of the tableclothless table, its top still steaming. I like sago pudding when it has been cooking in the oven for a long time as it goes soft and creamy and slides down easily. As Mother hands us each a bowl, for a time all that can be heard is the song of spoons as they clatter on the dishes. These days we are always hungry.

The gaslight has not yet been lit and the room is dark, just the fire glowing.

"It's looking a bit lighter out there," says Mother. "You two need to wrap up warm. Hurry up. You have to be there by six."

It doesn't take Jack long to get ready. His outdoor clothes are still in a pile on the mangle in the kitchen where he had dropped them when they were moved from Father's chair. He pulls on his balaclava and as

Mother tries to put a scarf around his neck, he shrugs her off, saying he isn't a baby.

I am different. Mother wraps me up from head to toe and when she has finished I can hardly breathe, never mind get cold. My red coat is now quite short so I have to wear leggings. It takes Mother some time to fasten the many buttons on the outside. My pixie-hood and scarf now firmly in place, I know why Jack didn't want a scarf. I am almost strangled. With gloves pushed onto my hands, we are ready to go.

"Just you look after your sister, Jack. Dorothy, you stay with Jack." With a last pull of my scarf, Mother opens the back door and we are released.

The snow goes up to the middle of my shoes. It covers the yard and though it is dark, the snow is sparkling white and it is so fresh that our feet make the first marks. We crunch our feet up and down. Jack picks up a load of snow and starts rolling it in his hands. As I breathe steam comes out of my mouth, like the smoke that comes from Father's pipe.

Just as Jack is about to throw the snowball at me, our Aunt Lily comes down the gitty. She lives in the house next to the house next door. She is one of Father's sisters and she doesn't like Mother. Father says that's nonsense, but Mother says it is because she is from the East End of London and refuses to go to Chapel. When we children go on Sunday, Father's sisters take us and Mother stays at home. She says that religion is not for her. Father has lots of sisters — Aunt Lily, Aunt Betty, Aunt Flo, Aunt Doris and Aunt Mabel — and three brothers: Uncle Frank, Uncle Arthur and Uncle Jim. Most of them live with Grandfather and Grandma Compton, right around the corner from us. Only tall Aunt Mabel lives outside the village, but we still see her quite a bit.

We crouch down and wait for Aunt Lily to walk along the pathway, hoping that she will pass. But she stops and grasps Jack's coat sleeve, pulling him towards her.

"Come on, you two," she commands. Whatever she says sounds razor-sharp, thin and snappy like her. "If you are coming to this carol singing we need to hurry."

Now we are on the Sheffield Road. It feels as though everything is still. I look up. The sky is bright, thousands of stars twinkle in blue-black velvet. The snow is like a carpet, thicker than one I've ever felt beneath my feet. Turning left, we head towards the back entrance to the Chapel. Aunt Lily soon leaves us to join some ladies who are trying to hurry along the opposite pavement. I can tell they are part of the Chapel choir by the size of their hats.

The snow down Chapel Street is no longer white, many feet having trodden it. Figures appear in the darkness beside the Chapel's arched side doorway and Mr Compton — the choirmaster, who I think is my relation, though he never acts like he is — is giving out instructions.

"Ladies and gentlemen! Through into the Sunday school room, if you please. Children, wait in the road."

A figure jumps out. It's George. "At last! Thought you weren't coming." He throws his arm around Jack's shoulder and they head off. It is so cold that I decide to ignore Mr Compton and go into the warm schoolroom to see if I can find my Aunt Flo. She is my favourite aunt, her hair is what Mother calls bobbed and she is pretty and dresses in what Mother calls "the latest fashions." She loves to do my hair and can do different things to it that aren't my usual plaits.

But as I go in, I get caught in a stream of ladies coming back outside. There is a strong smell of sherry, Grandma Compton's favourite drink. The ARP man, Mr Thompson, wearing his helmet and armband is telling them to get outside. "It is a serious matter of village security. I must . . ." he is saying urgently.

"Ladies and gentlemen," shouts Mr Compton, "could you please wait here by the door for a moment, there are a few issues to clear up."

"Quiet please," the ARP man's voice calls loudly. "And listen carefully. As you proceed from house to house, you must keep the lanterns you are carrying pointing downwards. Don't let the light shine up or you will be breaking all the blackout regulations."

A voice from behind him shouts that it's Christmas in Germany too. But this makes the warden puff himself up even more.

"Aye, Pete. I know it's Christmas and for now we've managed to stop the Huns from invading, but the Luftwaffe don't care. If they see a beacon of light, they will bomb it. I am here to protect you and as such you must obey all my instructions at any —"

At this moment, a snowball flies over and hits the ARP man on his helmet. Mr Compton says, not very harshly, "Boys, boys. We'll have no throwing of snow. Now, I am sure that you are all aware that our best bass singer is not with us. Let us take a moment to ask the Lord to care for Freddie Fretwell as he fights in this dreadful war. And for all our boys who lost their lives in the Battle of Britain."

Silence falls and even the boys are quiet. "Lord," continues the choirmaster, "we ask you to watch over our friend Freddie in his hour of need. We will miss him on this time of your Son's birth and ask you to send him back to us safely."

A chorus of "Amen!" rings out.

"So let us give it our best for Freddie!" shouts Mr Compton, his fist pumping the air. "Everyone know what we're singing?"

The soprano section of the choir starts warming up. The altos follow and I can hear Aunt Lily, her voice sharp and pointy. I feel an arm around my shoulders and Uncle Jim leans down.

"You all right there, young Dot? If you get cold, just come and find me or one of your aunts and we'll warm you up." Uncle Jim is always kind. He tries to make peace between Father and Uncle Arthur and Father and Grandfather Compton.

As we head back down Chapel Street for the main road, I find myself walking beside June. She doesn't come to our school, or play on the Miners' Recreation Ground because her mother says the children who play there are something called vulgars. June says I am not a vulgar and she is allowed to sit beside me at Sunday school. June has rosy cheeks and she is older than me and Father says she is a little bit posh.

Passing the entrance to the recreation ground, the column heads out of the village, down Sheffield Road and towards the coal mine. I have been down this road with Mother, when we have taken Bob in his pram to meet Father on his way home from work. We've never walked as far as the mine. It's a dark and dangerous place, says Father, and children are not allowed anywhere near. Jack and the gang have been trying to get anywhere near but get scared and run away. I never, ever want to see it. A few weeks ago Father had a terrible accident down the mine and was carried home on a board and was covered in blood. I thought he was going to die. But he didn't. One good thing about that accident, though, was that the next day Grandfather Compton gave us our four hens — Henry, Harry, Horace and Matilda — and since then we always have eggs to eat and share round.

Before we have gone anywhere near as far as the pit a halt is called.

"What's the matter, Tom?" shouts Uncle Jim. "Why we stopping?"

There is confusion in the line. I hear Mr Compton saying "sorry" a lot of times. He stands on the box he uses for conducting us.

"I was just asking if people wanted to start singing at the beginning of the houses, or walk down to the last house and work our way back. What do you think?"

"I think we should start at the bottom and work our way back, Tom. Might be better for the children."

Uncle Jim sighs the words: "He is a fusspot, that cousin of mine. I wonder how he ever manages to run a bank. If we don't hurry up, the pubs will be shut."

After what seems like a long time the column starts moving. We go through a green gate and crunch our way across the pebbles to a large house. A dog barks, a deep growly kind of bark, and a man shouts, "Casper! No! Get down!"

Aunt Lily pulls me forward and I find myself standing at the bottom of three steps. For a moment I panic. Why am I to stand here, so near the front? But I feel better when June appears beside me, along with Jack and George. There is a lot of commotion among the adults, people hissing to each other and a lot of pushing. Then the oil lamp — the one the ARP man warned us about — is lit and held high. I look up to check there are no Germans in the sky. Several ladies complain that they can't see the music.

"Ladies, please," says Mr Compton, and I wonder if he is going to cry. "We have to remember the regulation angle. Dorothy, June, will you please go and ring the bell."

A man, a glass in his hand, opens the large wooden door and steps onto the front step. Light shows behind him. A smart lady, a big boy and a girl, with beautiful hair that tumbles down her shoulders, come out behind him. She looks down her nose at June and I, her lips pushed out in a pout.

Mr Compton nods to the man and then we start to sing. It's "O Little Town of Bethlehem" and I know most of these words so I sing them as loudly as I can. We go straight into "Deck the Halls", the fa-la-las causing me a bit of trouble.

As we finish, the man claps the back of the hand that holds the glass, the lady smiles and claps, the boy looks up to the sky and the girl just stands. The dog has long since disappeared.

Next we sing a carol that I don't know. I am not sure if I have to keep quiet or pretend I know the words. The ladies are singing very high notes. Aunt Lily stands close behind me and she misses the high notes.

The man holds up his hand. "Thank you, Mr Compton. Splendid, splendid. May we take this opportunity to wish you and your, er singers, a Merry Christmas."

He comes down the steps and puts his hand on the top of my head.

"And now, I suspect you'll be on your way. Pretty cold out here and plenty of others waiting for you," he says, patting me quite hard.

Mr Compton makes himself look tall, pulls me from under the man's hand and marches me across the pebbles back the way we came. Everyone else follows. Mr Compton keeps up a steady stream of mumbles, though I can't catch much of what he says. Whatever it is doesn't sound as though it is full of goodwill.

We trundle through the gate and on to the road. It is very dark and very cold and I want to go back home, but then I remember last year. I let go of Mr

Compton's hand and try to find Harry to show him I am still here.

When we get to the next house, the man at the top of the steps is smiling. His door is open wide and, without missing a beat, the ladies pour up the stairs straight through the front door. June and I follow just in time to see a lady in a white lacy cap carrying a carpet out of the hallway. She drops a curtsey and disappears. There are lights on the Christmas tree and I can't stop looking.

We get into positions in the hallway and this time sing four carols, one after the other. I get lost during "In the Bleak Midwinter", recovering just in time for "poor as I am". They certainly aren't poor in this house. There are quite a few people watching us — the man who opened the door, he reads at Chapel; the lady who plays the organ; a very pretty young woman who wears a tight pale blue dress and has her hair piled high on her head; and a young man who is wearing a smart blue uniform. A grey-haired lady sits on the hall chair beside the young couple and a boy, a little older than me, sits on her knee. After each carol they all clap and when we get to "Jingle Bells", they all join in.

When we finish, the man thanks us and asks Mr Compton if we would care to stay for something to whet the coming of Christmas. It is just as well he says yes, as the two girls with lace caps and blue dresses come into the hallway with glasses on a tray. They all clink against each other and as they walk around the choir, all the ladies say, "No, I couldn't," but then they do and soon everyone is drinking and talking. Glasses

16

of fruit juice and jam tarts are passed to us children, and June and I look at the lights on the Christmas tree.

The young man in the uniform is talking to Uncle Jim. "I'm training to be a pilot," he says. "We need to get quite a few fighters into the air quickly if we are to beat the Luftwaffe, nippy chaps they are. Have you joined up yet?"

"Not yet. I'm down the mine," replies Uncle Jim. "Though I doubt it will be too long before they call me up."

When the glasses are empty and the chatter gets stiller, Mr Compton stands on his box.

"I think it might be time to move on," he tells us. "Before we go, may I, on behalf of the Chapel choir, thank you for letting us sing in your lovely house and for your kind hospitality." There is a big cheer from the choir and I shout loudly. Mother says we are singing at the posh houses and posh people aren't like us, but these people have been very nice to us. I run up to the lady and drop a curtsey.

Feeling Christmassy, we walk up into the village, stopping under the sign of the Crossed Keys.

"Well, here we are then, Tom," shouts Uncle Jim. "Let's nip in here for a sing-song."

For a moment no one speaks. The choir now fills the whole pavement and two miners, still wearing coal dust, weave past.

"You going in, me duck? We'll sing a few with you," laughs one of the men. He speaks right at Mrs Wood, the butcher's wife.

"Yes. Yes, we are," she says, and turning to the other ladies, she almost shouts, "Well, they are all God's creatures."

As everyone piles into the pub, Aunt Lily says:

"Heavens! Children can't come into a pub. We shall have to take them home."

But Mr Compton has poked his head inside the drinking bit. With his hat in his hand, he calls, "There's a small hallway behind the side door." He waves his hand towards the yard to show where the side door is. "The barman says that we can sing and the children can sing from this hallway, but they must not go anywhere where there is drinking."

So the decision is made. It takes quite a time to sort everyone out. The barman shouts that he is "not entertaining ladies in his bar" and all the adults cross the passageway and go through another door. Seven boys and June and I now stand in the hallway. It is not a very friendly place. All the walls are painted dark green from top to bottom and the floor is covered with red tiles, some of them broken. Now that all the adults have gone it is very quiet, and it is cold again. When the door to the bar is opened, a puff of warm smoky air comes into the hall and I can see coloured paper garlands hanging over the bar.

Soon we hear the adults sing, but it sounds silly when we try to join in. There is a chair in the hall and the boys start climbing on it and playing king of the castle. June gets kicked on the leg, she starts to cry. Jack shouts, "Get off the chair and let her sit down." But

June does not want to sit, she just cries louder and louder, "I want to go home."

A puff of warm air hits my legs. Aunt Flo looks shocked. "Tom! We'd better go, the children are getting cold out here." Now there is a jumble of people and the boys crowd forward trying to see into the drinking room. I spot some of the choir ladies putting down their drinking glasses before we see them. With thanks from both sides, the choir returns.

"Well, that was fruitful," says Mrs Wood, her face bright. "I think we should try another pub, don't you? But I do think it's time for the children to go home, Mr Compton."

Mr Compton blinks a lot and looks surprised that we are still here.

"They can see their own way home," says Aunt Lily. And with that we are off — Jack, George, Harry, Mike and me. I shout Merry Christmas to June. We walk until we turn the corner in the road, and then we run through the snow as fast as we can. At the bottom of the gitty we stop. I slip a few times and now I am tired.

"We'll call for Arthur," says Jack.

I try not to let my voice sound weepy because Harry will have something to say if I cry.

"I want to go home," I murmur.

All eyes look at me. Then I have an idea. "I want a tiddle."

The eyes still watch me, but it is agreed that everyone wants a tiddle "and girls can't do it up walls".

No one says anything, but we all make our way to my house. When Jack pushes open the door I can see the bike and I know that Father is home. The lovely smell of Christmas hits me and our home-made paper chains dance up and down on the ceiling.

Father is sitting in his armchair, pipe in hand, the old blanket protecting the chair from the coal dust. I want to jump on him, but I know not to, not until he is washed. Mother's voice is sharp.

"Leave your father alone; he's just come home from a double shift. If he stays down that hole much longer, he'll turn into a mole."

"So where have you lot been till this late?" He looks up at the railway clock, which has just clonked half past.

"We've been carol singing," Harry replies. "With the Chapel."

"Ah, yes. God bless you. Who was there? Any men?"

"Uncle Jim was there, and another man," I say. "And two old men I don't really know. Before we set off we had to say a prayer for a man called Freddie Fretwell."

"Oh, Freddie Fretwell. I heard he'd joined the army and gone away," Father says. "Let's hope him and that great bass voice come home soon.

"So how about you lot singing a cheery carol for me?" asks Father, his blue eyes twinkling.

He lays down his pipe and Mother sits down. After much mumbling and coughing we sing "Once in Royal David's City". Mike does the first bit, like I think an angel must sound, and then it goes downhill from there.

"That was beautiful!" Father claps loudly and Mother gives us one of her rare smiles. There is a

20

picture of her in the houseplace where she is smiling and pretty, a smile we don't see that often in real life. "I think that effort deserves a penny," she says.

Mother takes down her purse and gives the penny to Father. All the boys hold out their hands, but Father gives it to me.

"Let the woman look after the money, lads, and then you'll always have some."

Jack's eyes almost drill through my head.

"So shall we go and sing round the village now?" Harry asks cheerfully. "We'll take good care of Dot, Mrs Compton."

He can be such a turn-around, when he wants something, can Harry.

Mother tightens my scarf. "Jack, you bring her back in half an hour, do you hear me? It's gone half-past seven now, I want her back soon."

"I want a tiddle." I remember why I've come home.

"Well do it in the pail in the kitchen," she snaps. "I'm not going all the way down the garden with you."

Back out into the ice-cold dark air, it's hard to breathe and white clouds of steam rise from every face. We head to Bert and Arthur's house. The door opens before we get there, Arthur on the lookout for us, his coat buttoned up already.

"Where've you been?"

"Where's Bert?" asks George.

Bert's round face appears at the door. "I'm not coming, got a cold." He coughs into his hand to show how bad he is.

"Don't be out too long," says Mrs Baker. We don't see her very often now there is a war. Her husband got called up to the fight and she hasn't been well since he left. Mother is kind to her, maybe because Bert is kind to me.

We have made a plan. Jack says that as we have sung at the big houses we should now stick to the houses round the village green. Last year, when I was allowed to go for the first time, we ran into another gang carol singing their way down Crich Lane. Mother says that there are dozens of starving children living down dark alleyways off there and Father told us that because of something called the General Strike there aren't enough mines for all the miners and lots of people have no mines to go down any more and they all live there.

So we start with the row of houses where Bert and Arthur live. I want to start with our Grandma Compton, but Jack says that she will call us in and then we'll never get any money collected. The five of us gather in the doorway next to Bert and Arthur's house.

"What shall we sing?" I ask.

"Your dad said everyone likes 'Once in Royal David's City',' says Mike. "I can do my high bit too, if you like."

The boys decide it is better for me to ask for the money because they say it doesn't sound so cheeky if a girl asks. Or maybe they listened to my father.

We head up School Road, singing at doors that open into dark alleyways between houses. As soon as Mike sings we get a penny and so we ditch everything and go straight to Mike's solo. We pass the Black Boy public house, and hear the choir singing songs that don't much sound like carols to me.

After a while, I feel very tired and cold.

"I want to go home," I tell anyone who is listening, even Harry, but no one is. "I'm going home."

This time I poke Jack in the back. He turns. "All right, Dot. We'll go on without you. Head down Top Road and then down the gitty. Give us the pennies and we'll share them out. I'll bring yours home."

And then he is back with the boys. I trudge home. The snow is falling thick and fast.

The house is dark. I push the door open and with what feels like my last ounce of energy I fall in and shout out. I hear a ruffling from the bedroom and Father calls, "Hang on there, Dot." I stand in the kitchen, waiting for him to come down and help me take my outdoor clothes off. He comes down in his nightshirt.

"Look at you, Dollie," he says. "More snow. That's all we need, the boys working double time to get the coal up when they can't get it to the railway. The factories will close, never mind the war effort. Let's hope it's snowing in Germany. Better get you to bed."

Next morning, as we sit at the table eating our porridge, I ask Jack about the carol singing money.

"What money?" he asks.

Mother gives him a hard look.

"Give Dot her money, Jack."

He pulls a couple of pennies, a halfpenny and a farthing from his pocket.

"There you are," he says.

"Jack! Just you give Dot her fair share," Mother says, and stands over him until another penny is found.

It doesn't really matter how we share it because all the money that we have has to be spent on Christmas presents for Mother and Father. We have already looked in the village shop windows and seen a pair of bright suspenders for Father. When he puts on his best suit, Father always fastens bright suspenders around his legs and clips them to his black socks.

After we have played with Bob and helped Mother, we go down to the shops to buy the presents. The shops shut early on Christmas Eve and we see all the gang out doing the same thing. Jack and I go to the haberdashery shop and look at the price tag on the suspenders.

"If you give me a penny and that halfpenny and I add it to mine, we can afford them." Jack jingles the money in his pocket.

"But what about Mother?" I ask. "Have we got enough for her?"

We buy the suspenders and walk over to the hardware shop. There are lots of bottling jars on sale and so we buy her one of those. We have enough over to get Bob a tiny wooden car. I tell Jack we need to hurry back if there is to be enough time for Santa to take the presents so he can deliver them to Mother and Father.

As we struggle up the road, my arms wrapped carefully around the bottling jar, two men walk towards us. They are wearing blue overalls and carrying big bags. My heart seems to stop and I can't breathe. I

24

almost drop the jar as I grab Jack's sleeve and pull him towards me.

"What?" he shouts.

Still not moving, I nod towards the two men.

"Germans!" I hiss.

Jack spins round. "What do we do?" he whispers. A few weeks ago, after me and the gang had gone to explore the new military camp at the edge of the village and I had got through a hole in a hedge right into the grounds of the camp, some German prisoners of war had escaped. They had taken washing off Mrs Burton's line and dressed themselves in her and Mr Burton's clothes. Although they had been found and taken back, we think they had made a bid for freedom through the hole I had made bigger when I squeezed through it. We haven't told anyone, especially Constable White.

The men walk up to us.

"Excuse me, my love," says the taller one, not sounding very German. "I don't want to knock you over with this bag."

Smiling, he swings a large canvas bag past Jack's legs. "Merry Christmas! We'll be back to finish our work soon. Keep you all nice and safe, it will," he says kindly.

We both go down like burst balloons.

"Merry Christmas," says Jack, a little sadly.

"What do you think they are doing?" I ask Jack.

"I don't know, Dot. But we'll look out for them after Christmas and keep an eye on them. The main thing is they are gone now."

As we head back home, I think Christmas is Christmas and whatever is happening or happens, we must finish this job in hand and get the presents to Santa.

That is, if he hasn't been captured, or bombed.

I run after my brother.

CHAPTER
TWO

Has Santa been?

Christmas Eve 1940

Not long to wait now. One more sleep and Christmas will be here. This morning I asked Father how we will know when the war is over, what happens if it's finished and we just haven't found out yet, and he said, "Dot. I'll know. And I will tell you as soon as I know."

I look up at the fairy on top of our tree. Mother has used a shiny sweet paper to decorate the star at the end of our tiny fairy's wand. "Maybe our fairy can work some magic for us and end this war," I say to Father, though in my heart I know it isn't that straightforward.

While Mother is spooning her home-made strawberry jam into her pastry cases, I take one from the baking tray so that she will tell me off and not notice Jack smuggling the bottling jar from underneath the sink to behind the mangle.

"Dorothy!" she slaps my hand. "Leave those jam tarts alone, there'll be nothing left for Christmas Day."

It's worked. Jack has made it out without her noticing. Now for the next part of our plan.

"We've got a present for Father," I say. "Can you get it to Santa before tomorrow morning for us?" I show her the brown paper bag with Father's new garters. She forgets to be cross with me and takes a little peek into the bag.

"Oh! That's very nice."

One of her special smiles lights her face as she pushes her hair back behind its band and wipes her hands down her apron. "Do you want them sent in the bag or out of it?"

"Out of the bag," I reply. "Do you think you'll be able to get them to Santa this evening, or are we too late?"

Mother pulls me close and gives me one of her rare hugs. It must be Christmas!

"You're never too late to get lovely presents to Santa. Come here," she says as Jack walks through the curtain. As my brother gets pulled into the hug, he gives me a thumbs-up. He wiggles himself out of her hold.

All the Christmas food is ready. The two puddings sit in their basins on the wooden copper top, wrapped in the white cloth. Next to them is the large washing-up bowl. I stand on tiptoe and peer over to look at the red jelly wobbling in a glass basin in its middle.

"Cost me almost all our ration coupons did these, Dolly," says Mother, showing me two small tins. "But it's Christmas and we've earned them."

"What are they?" I ask. There is a picture of small golden half-moons floating about.

"They're called orange segments and they taste lovely with a bit of jelly."

Mother strokes the tin as she puts it down. I think they must be made of gold.

"And I got this." She holds the other tin, which has a picture of a fish on it. I shudder. The only other thing I have seen with a fish on its label is the cod liver oil bottle. Mother makes me take a spoonful every night and I hate it. But Mother is looking lovingly at this fish on a tin.

"It's pink salmon, Dolly. And it means that now we have no coupons left until next month."

Touching the tin, Mother sighs. "Oh, I do hope that siren doesn't go off tonight, or tomorrow. Won't make for a peaceful Christmas if we're constantly in and out."

"Don't the Germans have Christmas holidays?" I ask.

"Yes, Dolly, I think Santa Claus starts off from there, all the German children will be waiting for him too. But it is not the children and their mothers who will send the bombs. It is mad men full of hate." She raises her apron to her face as a tear escapes.

Bob tries to look at the food, almost pulling over the bowl with the water in it.

Mother is back to herself. "Get out of here, all of you, before something happens!"

Jack does not need telling twice; he is out and off snowballing. I take Bob into the warm houseplace and sit him on the pegged rug. He curls up next to me and as we look into the crackling, glowing fire, he soon falls asleep, his warm body making me yawn. But as I am drifting into a dream, I jolt awake, remembering the

Christmas card I need to finish for Grandma and Grandfather Compton.

I lower Bob down gently on to the rug and get my pencils and the half-finished card from the cupboard. I have drawn a Christmas tree and presents underneath it and a window so you can see the snow falling outside and as many of our family — including most of my aunts and uncles — as I can fit in. It's not easy to tell who everyone is, so I try my best. Grandfather Compton has bubbles coming from his mouth due to his bubbly voice, brought on by too much Thin Twist, according to Mother; Grandma Compton has a big mixing bowl in her arms and her blue-and-white apron on as she is always baking — Mother says she can make sawdust and nettle stew smell good; Aunt Flo has her bob; Aunt Lily always has her hair in a tight bun; Aunt Mabel is dressed smart as she works somewhere that means she has to dress nicely; Aunt Doris has two front teeth that make her look like a rabbit; Aunt Betty is short and plump, like Mother; Uncle Frank has a dimple in his chin; Uncle Arthur always has a laugh in his voice, so I draw him smiling, though he doesn't always say nice things; and Uncle Jim is very strong and has big, square shoulders even though he is short like most of his brothers and sisters. Mother is smiling in my picture and has her hair loose from her band and she is pretty, and I make Father look like a handsome prince, his yellow-orange hair like a crown. Jack is tall and thin and straight up, and Bob is just a mass of smiling blond curls and chubby arms and legs.

As I make my hair long and yellow — loose over my shoulders like the girl at the big house where we went carol singing — I think about Christmas Day. Just one more sleep. I have waited for this day for such a long time, and even though there is a war on, I am excited. Tonight is the night when the fairies come here to us, the night when Santa Claus lets bright shining magic come to all the children. I close my eyes and make a wish to fairies everywhere. Please let Santa leave toys for all the children in the world, even in Germany, especially in our village.

I can hear Miss Mallory's words in my head. "Don't forget, children," she said, "whatever Santa manages to bring you, do say a big thank you to him. He has had to travel across countries where guns are firing and he won't be able to stop at some children's houses because they have been blown up. So say a little prayer for these children who live in the shadow of war whenever you can."

I sit at the table and look down at the card. I'd better say a prayer now. I'm not sure if I should say it to Jesus or to Santa, so I include them both.

And suddenly the thought hits me. How is Santa Claus going to get down our chimney with this large fire at its bottom?

"Mother?" I call. "How will Santa get down the chimney with the fire still burning?"

"Your father has made arrangements for Santa to come down the kitchen chimney," she says as she leans over the fireguard. She is holding a black rod in her oven gloves which she uses to raise the lid of the boiler.

31

"He got a sweep to brush it a couple of weeks ago." Disappearing into the kitchen she returns with the ladle and pours water into the boiler.

"Let's hope that warms up in time," she says, closing the lid. "You three have got to have your bath tonight. Your father will have to wait for his Christmas bath till the water has warmed up again. Won't be enough for me, as usual." She heads back to the kitchen mumbling to herself: "Don't suppose he will mind going to the Black Boy with his dirt on."

As if on cue, the outside door opens and Father arrives home, bringing a great waft of cold with him. His feet stamp on the doorstep and I hear crashing metal as he kicks snow from his bicycle wheels.

"I tell you what," he calls from the kitchen, "it's blooming cold out there. We've had some more snow. And look who I found snowballing his way to Christmas!"

Mother is at the ready. "Don't you two come in here in those wet clothes. Get them off in there, and don't knock that food."

We all know that she is talking to Jack, but Father replies, "Oh, I will Nellie and I won't Nellie and a Merry Christmas to you as well."

His eyes sparkle out of his coal-dusted face. We are all pleased to see him. Even our home-made red, white and blue paper chains dance up and down on the ceiling when he comes in, and the fire sparks and crackles. We know that now the fun will start. Often when Mother sounds cross, as if she has too much to do and not enough time to do it in, Father has a way of making her laugh and feel better.

Having removed his boots, but still in his dirty work clothes, he comes into the houseplace, picks her up and swings her around.

"Joe! Stop it!" she shouts. "You're all dirty and you'll knock the food off." But before she has time to say more he kisses her and she is still and I see her hand push his worn and filthy cap over his eyes.

He puts her down and removes the cap. "Stop it, you silly devil!" she says, but the anger and worry are gone from her face.

"Thank goodness that's over for a couple of days," says Father as he ruffles my hair and holds his other hand out to Bob. "Quite a few going in on Boxing Day. They're trying to clear the yard so they can get the coal to the rail trucks. It's no good us going in if we can't get more coal out." He speaks between puffs as he lights his pipe, his mug of tea steaming on the chair arm. It will take more than Christmas, or Germans, to break this routine.

Mother grunts. She hasn't time for mine talk. Christmas still fills her mind. "Better put some fire in the kitchen, Joe. Bath time tonight."

"Oh, Nellie. Let me finish this pipe first." Father holds out his pipe to let Mother know which pipe he wants to finish smoking. He sits contentedly as he puffs on it and for a while, as we wach the clouds of smoke, there is peace and stillness in the room. I gaze at Father and think about the garters that Santa will deliver for him.

★   ★   ★

And then it gets busy. Supper time followed by bath time, after which it will be nearly Christmas.

"Sit on that settee," Mother commands as she pulls the pegged rug back and puts it under the table. Armed with the metal dustpan and the long fire poker, Father heads for the fire. Pushing the dustpan firmly into the fire, he scrapes as much fire as he can onto the dustpan and takes the glowing coals into the kitchen. The sulphur smell of coal burning fills the room and we watch as Mother carries the empty coal bucket into the kitchen and closes the curtain behind her. The red coals will be sulky in the kitchen fire grate — they never like to be moved. We sit still. Any movement from us children can be dangerous. As Father tells us, a fire well managed means that Mother can cook, the water can heat and we can be warm.

After Father has finished bringing coal from outside to build up the fire in the houseplace again — already the room is cold — Mother asks if Father wants his supper now.

"No thanks, Nellie," he replies. "I'll wait until I've had my bath. What have I got?"

"Managed to get you some tripe. It had just come in. I was lucky."

I look at Father to watch him smile. He always enjoys his tripe with pepper and vinegar on it.

"That smells nice, Mother," says Jack as we watch her take brown pasties from the oven.

"I got a tin of Spam, so I made some pasties with all the bits of leftover pastry and a bit of Spam. If you put the cloth on, you three can have your tea now. That'll give the fire time to burn through before you have your bath."

We are to the table in quick time. "Are those hands washed?" asks Mother, as Father looks longingly at the pasties.

"I could murder one of those, Nellie," he says.

As we three go to wash our hands, Mother passes him one. Tossing it from hand to hand, he sinks back into his chair.

"Father didn't have to wash his coaly hands," I hiss to Jack as the cold water makes me shiver.

"Wouldn't make any difference," says Jack. "He's so dirty."

As we eat, we listen to Christmas carols on the wireless. For tonight the war is forgotten. Father has a good voice and he sings all the carols with gusto, only stopping when a young boy's voice sounds, clear as a bell ringing, and then a choir joins him. Mother loves her music. She seems to rest only when the music plays on the wireless on Saturday night. Now, she sinks on to the settee. Father places his finger to his lips and all is silent. We know to give Mother her moment of peace.

When the carol ends, Mother is back on her feet.

"Right. Bath time! Everyone to the lavatory!"

As we start to say we don't need the toilet, Father pushes us to the back door. He tells us that Santa's elves only visit children who have been to the lavatory and have had their baths. We put on our shoes and coats.

"I go snowballing, I go snowballing," shouts Bob happily.

The snow is quite deep. Father walks in front. He has put on his big boots and he sluthers his feet to make a narrow pathway for us to walk along. Mother follows, holding a lighted candle. The wind is like ice. Father checks the lavatory to make sure none of our next-door neighbours are in it and that it isn't frozen over, but the sacking he has wrapped around the pipes has worked and after Jack goes first, the lavatory flushes. It feels like hours later that we walk back, Father carrying Bob, who is quiet now he has been allowed to throw a snowball at each of us.

As we reach the door, Father takes the big tin bath from the wall outside the houseplace window and bangs the snow off it. He carries it into the houseplace and Mother sets to wiping it with a cloth. The smell of bleach fills the room. It is bath time! I am so cold that I can't wait to feel the warm water cuddle me. Once again, we three sit on the settee as Father and Mother make this possible.

Mother, ladle in hand, empties the boiler at the side of the fire and the bath fills up, the water hissing as it hits the tub. It would take too long for it to cool down, so Father has to carry cold water from the kitchen in the big enamel washing-up bowl and splash it in. After three more trips, Mother swishes her hand around the water. "It's ready," she says.

I help Bob undress and take my clothes off as quickly as I can. Jack waits. He doesn't like us to see him with no clothes on any more. Father tickles Bob and squeals of laughter fill the room. We go first. Sinking into the warm, clean water is one of my favourite things.

"Are you going up to the Black Boy?" Mother asks as she pours cold water into the boiler.

"Aye. Might go up for half an hour. Jack Mills's eldest has joined up. He's going away after Christmas. Think I'd better have a pint with him."

Mother opens a drawer in the dresser, lifts out her purse and hands it to Father.

"Don't stay all night, Joe, will you? Wish the lad well from me. Tell him to take good care of himself. And wish all the lads a happy Christmas."

Kissing each of us, he winks at me. "If I see Santa out there I'll tell him you're all in bed and asleep, so you had better hurry off upstairs before he gets here."

And whistling "Good King Wenceslas," he is gone.

"Right," says Mother, in what doesn't sound like too festive a voice, "let the cleaning commence." She holds out a block of carbolic soap.

First Bob is scrubbed, his curly hair straightened with the weight of the water as Mother ladles it over his head. She pulls him out and rubs him down with a rough towel — my least favourite bit — puts a clean nightshirt over his head, combs his hair and sits him on the settee. He looks like a wet angel. He never makes a fuss. Unlike me.

Without speaking, Mother dips the ladle into the bath water and pours it over my head. My plaits have been undone and now my long hair hangs wet over my face. Gasping for breath, I try to push the hair from my face. I know worse is to come. With my head pushed backwards and my hair thrown back, the large block of carbolic soap hits my head. I feel every movement as it rocks around my head. Mother has a thing about me catching nits in my long hair, so the lather and the scrubbing go deep and last long. I squeeze my eyes closed, but no matter how hard I try, the soap stings my eyes. I can't keep quiet any longer.

"It's in my eyes! It's in my eyes!" I scream.

But Mother has ways of controlling me with my long hair. "Sit still, Dorothy! Do you *want* nits? I certainly don't want them in my house, I've got enough to do at Christmas without worrying about them."

She gives my scalp another good scrub. I can't see what's happening, but now I wait for the water to gush over my head, and after what seems a long time, it comes. As I manage to start breathing again, Mother pulls me up by my hair and wrings water from it, like she wrings water from clothes.

"Come on, Jack, in you get. I want you all in bed in half an hour."

Mother rubs my hair so hard, I can hardly stand up. I can hear Jack though.

"Ugh. This water is *freezing!*"

Mother throws him the soap.

"Rub that on yourself. That'll warm things up."

Now the final agony starts. With all that rough treatment, my hair is full of knots. With my head backwards and my hair hanging before the now bright fire, Mother sits on the settee and starts to comb. For each lug she lifts my hair, twists it and combs it until it is pulled straight.

Wearing a clean nightdress, I sit on the settee beside Bob, who has fallen fast asleep. Jack has been rubbing the soap up and down one arm, but now he is covered in lather. And then he gets the same treatment — the cold water, the rough towel — and he comes out red and gleaming like us.

As I wait for him to get dry, I wonder where the lad who Father is having a drink with is going. Germany, I suppose. Then I remember Santa has to go to the German children before he comes to us. I wonder what Germany is like. I think it must be horrid. I wonder if there are many children there and, if there are, then maybe it can't be so bad. I wonder, if their fathers have gone away, how there are lots of children this Christmas night who will have to go to sleep not knowing where their fathers are, not able to give them presents or sing carols with them. It makes me sad. And then I wonder if it is right to be sad for the enemy and if children can be the enemy.

And then I have another thought. What happens if Santa gets captured by the Germans and then a German soldier takes Santa's clothes and, pretending to be Santa, comes down our chimney in his place? Suddenly I am terrified.

But how could a German soldier drive the sleigh? The reindeers wouldn't go with him. I am sleepy and as Mother hands me a mug of warm, milky Ovaltine, I tell myself to stop worrying.

Mother takes two hot bricks out of the oven and wraps each one in a piece of blanket to warm Bob's cot and Jack's bed. She wraps the iron oven shelf — still warm from all the cooking — in a piece of blanket for my bed. She gives them to Jack to carry upstairs.

"Have I got to go to bed at the same time as Bob?" moans Jack.

"If you want Santa to come, you do," says Mother.

"I need to leave Santa something to eat," says Jack. "And his reindeer will want something."

Mother is busy sorting out the dirty clothes and the towels. "Your father and I will do it after the bath has been emptied. Now up to bed, all of you, or Santa won't be coming at all."

I lie still on the warm patch in my bed. I am determined to stay awake and listen out for Santa. Santa, who will not be a German in disguise. If he does decide to come down the houseplace chimney, he will come down the chimney that passes through my bedroom. And if — as I hope he does, so he doesn't get burnt — he comes down into the kitchen, then he will pass by Jack. So one of us should definitely hear him.

When I wake up, the window is shining white. For a moment I lie and look at it, and then it hits me. It's here! Now! No more waiting. I creep out of bed, past Mother and Father. Jack is standing on the landing. Without a word and as silently as we can, we slide down the stairs. The stair-foot door squeaks. We freeze but no sound comes from above.

The kitchen is dark and cold, no sign of Santa there. The little fire that Father lit last night has gone out.

There is a piece of paper in the pot. "*Thank you, that was very nice*," Jack reads in a whisper. "He must have come down this chimney and eaten Mother's jam tarts in here!"

We creep through the green curtain into the house-place. The big fire glows red, sparks shooting up the chimney.

"Look, Dot," Jack says. "Look over there! He's been!"

We tiptoe over to the table. My legs are shaking. I know there is a war and this isn't a time to ask for things, but if Santa has brought me a doll, I will be good every single day, for ever. A line of presents runs down towards the fire. The first thing I see is one of Father's socks, fat and full. I put my hand inside and pull out a rosy apple and then some tuffies in shiny paper, a whole range of glimmering colours. Something hard lies in the toe of the sock. Hazelnuts!

And then, I nearly fall over. She is there! The doll I wrote and asked Santa for. Her fair curls are tucked into a knitted blue bonnet and her pink hands peep out beneath a matching coat.

"Dot!" hisses Jack. "Roller skates!" His voice is trembling.

As I look up, I see Father standing at the curtain. "Look! Santa's been."

"I can see, Dolly," replies Father, his voice all croaky, "but do you two know it's five o'clock in the morning?"

"Can't we stay up and play?" Jack's voice sounds pleading as Father holds the curtain high for him to pass through.

"No, Jack. It's too early. But you can take one thing back to bed with you."

"I'll take the roller skates!" Jack almost shouts.

"Take the book," says Father, pointing to the table. "You'll get hurt if you lie on roller skates. They'll be here when we get up later. Dot, you can take your doll."

Without waking Bob we three creep back up the stairs. I slide under my blankets; the bed is still warm. I watch my father slide his legs into his bed before tucking my doll in, and right then I am the happiest girl in the whole world.

And then it is the real morning and we can be noisy and excited. I am surprised at how shiny my doll's eyes look, and when I walk around the table towards her the eyes seem to follow me. I lift her carefully. She feels quite heavy, much heavier than my old rag doll, Millie Molly Mandy, who Father said I had to give to the Brown children. Putting her over my shoulder, the way Mother used to carry Bob when he was a baby, I take her to the settee. I look her all over. Her knitted coat, hat and dress are blue, the same colour as the jumper that Bob used to wear. As I tip her up on my knee to see if she is wearing any knickers, her eyes follow me.

"Don't mess about with her eyes, Dot, else you will break them," says Father. "They're special. They can move as you move her head."

"Can she see?" I ask.

"I suppose so," says Father.

Mother says that the bottling jar is the nicest she has ever owned and Father has promised to wear the garters today. Our Christmas breakfast makes everyone cheerful. Mother cooks some of the tomatoes from Grandfather's greenhouse that I helped put into large bottles last summer, and we have them on toast and we are all allowed to dip our bread in the bacon fat from Father's Christmas Day bacon. It's a pity the hens have stopped laying eggs for the winter, but we still have one or two left that Mother and I slid into a jar containing clear gluey-looking stuff that has been closed up under a bench in the pantry to keep them fresh. "One egg between us," Mother mumbles as it sizzles over the fire in the bacon fat. "What will this war do to us next?"

Father puts his arm round her shoulders. "We are still here together to eat it, Nellie. There are many who are not with their families this Christmas." He kisses the top of her head and she takes hold of his hand.

"When is this lot going to end, Joe? Haven't enough men died already?"

"When we stop them from spreading their poison, Nellie. It will take some time now we're fighting all those Italian soldiers in Egypt."

After breakfast, dressed in our Sunday-best clothes — Father clean and smart in his black suit and crisp white shirt — the four of us set off for a walk around the green. Mother stays at home to cook the Christmas dinner. Down the gitty the snow has turned to mud and we have to walk with special care in our school shoes. The pavement is so slippery and I can't hold Father's hand as I have my doll in my arms and I also have Grandma's Christmas card to carry. As we reach Grandma Compton's house, I climb the three stone steps, and Father pushes open the door and pulls the curtain aside. The warm air, the delicious smell of

Grandma Compton's cooking and the tick of my grandfather's grandfather clock greet us.

"Dolly! Merry Christmas!" says Aunt Betty, always on the move even if there is nowhere to move to. "What did Santa bring you?" She comes out of the kitchen holding a saucepan. I have my new doll in my arms and hold it out towards her. The doll looks at my aunt.

"Isn't she lovely," she says, moving back towards the kitchen. "Go on in and show your grandma."

Grandfather comes from the kitchen wearing his coat and muffle. Uncle Arthur, Uncle Frank and Uncle Jim are close behind.

"Coming for a drink, Joe?" asks Uncle Arthur.

"No, I've got the children, Arthur." Father is not very fond of this brother. I heard him say he doesn't like the way he thinks, especially when he said the Germans coming might do us good. But there is no argument today as it's Christmas.

"Could leave them here." Uncle Jim glances around to find his sisters.

"No thanks, Jim," says Father. "We just called in to show what Santa brought."

Father nods towards Jack, who holds up his precious roller skates. Uncle Arthur walks around the table to admire them.

"Oh!" he exclaims. "These the second-hand ones you got from Bill's attic? Came up well, didn't they?"

I look at Father and see a flash of anger. Then he smiles.

"No, Arthur, these are the ones that Santa brought down the chimney last night."

Grandfather squeezes past, pats Bob on the head and nods at Father. He and Father do not speak to each other. I once heard Father tell Mother that Grandfather Compton had hit Grandma, and he would never forgive him.

Grandma bustles into the room, her sleeves rolled up and a saucepan in her hands. She is, as always, wearing her blue-and-white apron. I duck out of the way as she heads for the fire, which burns as big and bright as ours. Puffing quietly, she rearranges the pans over the fire, opens the oven door, slides a pan out and then back in again. Her face is red and, smiling, she turns to us and holds her arms out.

"Come and give me a big Christmas hug, my lovelies." The doll takes up a lot of room, but Grandma Compton can give big hugs and kisses. "If you three look on the Christmas tree, I think you'll find some sugar pigs. Is it all right for them to eat them, Joe?"

Grandma makes the best sugar pigs in the world. Now she turns and kisses Father's cheek. He takes a white box from his pocket and passes it to her. "From all of us, Mother. Merry Christmas," he says. With a sugar pig in my hand I remember that I also have a present for Grandma.

"Oh and I made you this for you," I say as I hand the card over.

"Did you make this, Dot?" she asks, all surprised. "Aren't you clever. Is that me?" I go over and point out who everyone is. Then Grandma opens the box.

"Oh, they are lovely, Joe. Thank Nellie for me. I'll bring her something tomorrow." She holds the box out to show us some very white lace handkerchiefs embroidered with roses.

Father passes over three paper bags to his sisters. Soap. I heard the lady in the Co-op say that everyone is buying soap this year for Christmas, in case the country runs out.

"So what is the name of this new dolly then?" asks Aunt Flo as she turns to me.

"She only arrived this morning. She hasn't got one yet."

Aunt Flo takes her from me and looks into her eyes.

"Seeing as she has come this Christmas, maybe you should call her Hope."

Out of the house we head for the four lanes end — or as we call it, the Falling Ends — we pass the house where the thin children who worry Father live. Mother has made them some extra pudding and Father tells us he will bring it to them later. I look at their door and wonder if Santa knows that children live here. They wouldn't have had anything to leave him and his reindeer. Maybe I should give them my shiny sweets.

At the Falling Ends, Old Stan is sitting on the wooden bench beside the chemist's shop. My father gives him a small green carton. Mother sometimes has one of these — she says a Woodbine helps calm her nerves. Stan looks up at Father and tries to stand, but he only has one leg and has to use a big stick. He lost a leg fighting a war in France, a war Mother says was as bad as the one we are having now. The stick falls over and he sits down with a bump.

"You're a gent, lad, you're a gent."

Stan points his stick at the church over the road.

"Used to ring these bells at Christmas, didn't they, Joe, but no more." He takes a cigarette from the packet. Father strikes a match and offers him a light.

The teacher told us that if we heard the church bells ringing, wherever we were, we had to get home as quickly as possible because it would mean that the German soldiers have landed in Britain. There is a lot of talk about these Germans coming here. I don't want them to come, and I know Mother doesn't want them here, she has said so many times.

"Aye, Stan," says Father quietly. "We don't want them to ring now, do we."

We pass people going to the church. When we were at Grandma's house, Aunt Doris asked Father if we were going up to the service at the Chapel. "No, Doris," he replied gently. "Nellie wants us to stay at home with her today. They went carol singing a couple of days ago."

We wish the churchgoers a Merry Christmas as we head up School Road. It is quite a steep climb. Father carries Bob and holds my hand. Jack tries to slide his way up the hill, but after he has fallen twice and made his socks dirty, Father tells him to walk properly. As we reach the Black Boy, Father looks at its door for a little time and suddenly pushes Jack and I past a low wall and into its small yard.

"Wait there for one moment. Jack, Dot, watch Bob. I need to wish the boys a Merry Christmas."

Hanging tightly to Hope, I tidy her hair and redo the buttons on her dress. Then the sound of men's voices rises and Father is back with us. Wiping his hand across his mouth, he straightens his hat and picks up Bob.

"Homeward!" he says merrily.

Home is warm and welcoming and smells good — meat and potatoes roasting in the oven and something boiling noisily on the fire. Father stops by the door.

"Nellie, you know that extra pudding that you made, shall I get it down to Mrs Brown before I take my coat off?"

"Oh yes, Joe! I almost forgot. But don't hang around. Dinner is nearly ready."

As he leaves, she turns back to us. "What did your grandma have to say?" she asks.

We tell her how much she loved the lacy handkerchiefs and about the sugar pigs and Hope's new name, and she tells us to remind Father to take them out of his pocket. But when he comes back, the pigs are gone.

"I gave them to the Brown children," he says, as he passes Mother his good black coat, and pushes up his white sleeves. "Didn't look as if they were having much of a Christmas. Nellie, she said to thank you for your kindness. The children were clambering around the basin before the door closed."

I look around me. The fire crackles, Hope sits on the settee beside my new book, my shining sweets stand on the table in the corner by the fire and the Christmas tree shivers. On the ceiling Santa's green and blue fairies are dancing. I know that only I can see them, and as they flash their wings and tell me that the Brown children love the pink sugar pigs, I smile.

CHAPTER
THREE

Death is black

March 1941

The snow is melting fast. Mother's snowdrops are popping up in patches of garden. Soon there will be happy yellow daffodils around the green. But the village is gloomy. At the shops, in the Chapel, coming home after school, I see women standing together, their arms around each other.

On Saturday we are standing in the queue at the Co-op when a woman bangs the door open. She takes her place behind us and I can hear her crying quietly to herself. Mother turns round.

"Bad news, Fanny?" she asks.

"Our Bill got his papers yesterday. He's got to go away in a couple of weeks," she says, her voice wobbling. "Oh, Nellie. His mam already lost all her brothers in the last war. Now she thinks she's going to lose her only son."

Mother puts her arms around her and the two of them stand there rocking gently.

The woman behind the counter nods her head sideways towards the door at the back of the shop.

"Him who works at the back got his as well. Gone up to the office to see what to do. Don't know who will do his job when he goes."

I don't know what papers are, but no one seems to want them. Last night when he came home from the mine, Father told Mother that Grandma Compton can't stop crying because Uncle Jim has got his papers.

On the way home, Mother is quiet. The papers must be something to do with the war. Everything is to do with the war. As we come through the back door with the shopping, Father has the wireless playing, listening to the news.

"Shh . . ." He holds up his hand. "London has taken another pounding."

Mother looks worried. Grandma and Grandpa Burns live in London, serving fish and chips from their shop in Whitechapel. Mother has written to them to get them to come and stay with us, but they don't want to leave.

Later, as Jack and I toast our bread in front of the fire, I ask him what the papers are and why all the women are crying about them. "Are the men crying too?" I ask. Jack likes to tell me things about the war, and while I am not sure he is always telling the truth, he is sometimes the only one who will answer my questions.

He puffs himself up. "They're letters, Dot, sent through the post, telling men they have to join the army and go to fight the war. Father won't get any 'cos he has to stay on at the mine. He's too important for the King to lose. He's in charge of the putting the props in and laying out the face."

I let out my breath.

A few days later we watch as Uncle Jim goes off in a lorry, along with lots of other men in the village. He only has a small suitcase with him as he told Jack that he'd be getting a uniform so wouldn't be needing much from home. Grandma has given him two slices of barm bread and he is pushing them into his mouth as he walks down the road. I recognise the man from the Co-op, the man who works in the hardware store at the top of School Street and Mr Brown, the man whose children ate our sugar pigs at Christmas. There are a lot of women with their arms around each other and I can hear a lot of crying. Some of the men look very sad, but they aren't crying. Some look brave and strong, and some, like Uncle Jim, even look cheerful. A girl from my class at school is being hugged by her father as if he never wants to let her go.

"Come on, boys," shouts a voice from the lorry. "Let's jump to it! The Germans won't wait."

As the lorry drives away, we run after it, jumping and waving.

"Come back soon, Uncle Jim!" I shout.

"Kill the Germans!" shouts Jack.

Father and Aunt Lily have to hold up Grandma Compton on the way back to her house. We aren't allowed to come in. Grandma Compton doesn't like us to hear her crying that noisily.

A few days later, when I come home from school, Mother is drinking a cup of tea outside, talking to Mrs Parker, the lady who lives on the other side of the gitty.

Father says Mrs Parker and her family don't have two pennies to rub together and, when she can, Mother hands over our worn-out clothes.

Mrs Parker is crying. I used to be frightened if grown-ups were crying, but now that is all they seem to do. I wonder if Mr Parker has his papers.

"He wasn't going to die in some silly country," Mrs Parker is saying through her tears. "Said they'd have to catch him before they'd make him go in the army."

"Where's he gone, Tess?" asks Mother softly.

"I don't know, Nellie," says Mrs Parker, her voice wobbling. "He said it was better we didn't know. He can't come back until the war is over. How am I going to get food on the table for the little ones?"

Mother puts her arms around Mrs Parker. She tells her we will send something over later and the two of them stand together for a long, long time. I hear Mother crying and I turn and go back home. This time their sadness makes me sad and I want to find Jack so he can tell me what Mr Parker has done.

Jack tells me that it must mean that Mr Parker didn't want to fight and has run away to hide so that the men in the army can't find him. I ask him what will happen if the men from the army find Mr Parker, but Jack doesn't know.

Later, as Father is standing at the sink, washing coal off his face, Mother tells him about Mr Parker. He stops still, his hands frozen in mid-air, and he looks at her as if he has had more than the shock of the icy water.

"They'll catch him," Father says. "And when they do, they'll put him in prison. Or in a military camp. And then he'll wish he'd gone when they'd asked him. Woe betide him, Nellie. Woe betide him."

"And I say, good luck to him, Joe," says Mother. "I just hope he can come home soon."

Spring comes to the village — well, at least it has stopped raining — and we see the sun again and Mother's daffodils are starting to open. One morning when I am woken up by Mother getting out of bed in the pitch-dark, I wonder what is going on. I creep down the stairs after her.

"What do you think has happened?" Mother is asking as she fills the kettle.

Father is undoing his boots in the kitchen.

"Don't know, Nellie. But she seemed in a bit of a hurry. It's not every day you see our district nurse rushing around." I watch Father as he removes his working clothes. He went to the pit last night when I went to bed and it looks as though he has just come home. I wonder if there has been an accident.

"Old Mrs Allsop's been bad for a long time. Haven't seen her out and about for an age," Mother says from the houseplace as she puts the kettle onto the fire. "Do you think that son of hers has managed to go for some help for her?"

As Father hangs up his coat he almost bumps into me.

"Dolly! What are you doing up this early?" he says.

"Has there been an accident?" I ask, sleepy again.

"No, Dolly. It's old Mrs Allsop. She's needing the nurse. Go back to bed and we'll tell you what's to do in the proper morning."

Upstairs, I lie in my warm bed, Hope next to me, and think about Mrs Allsop. She lives in a row of little houses near to the Co-op. Last summer, when it was very hot, she sat out on a chair by her front door. As we passed her, Mother always said good-day. She never said good-day back, but she did raise her hand and nod. She is so large that I always stare at her, wondering how she didn't break the chair she was squashed on. She lives with her son, who wears the same hat on his head, winter or summer, and who, every day, heads for the bus to Rompton carrying a small black bag, returning, as Mother told me, "at four thirty on the dot, Dot". No one has ever heard him talk and no one knows what he does. Arthur says we should follow him one day so we can see where he goes. He has very big feet and his mouth hangs open and some people call him Slop. But I don't want to because he makes me feel a bit unsure. I try not to think about Mrs Allsop's son.

In the morning, Father is lying on the settee. He isn't asleep but he is dozing.

"Come on, Dorothy," says Mother, "we can leave Bob with Jack. Walk up to the Co-Op with me. We'll go early before the queue gathers. And we can see what's to do with Mrs Allsop."

As we come round the corner to the Co-op, there's a crowd of women standing together. But this time they haven't got their arms around each other. Instead they are looking up at Mrs Allsop's house. Her front door stands open and the district nurse's bike leans against the wall. A black car is parked at the pavement edge. Mother stops to ask what is happening. I squeeze between two women so I can see into the house.

I can see mounds of old clothes, piles of newspapers and lots of rubbish. The room is full of stuff and I don't see how anyone can fit inside the house. A very smart-looking man comes out on to the pavement and the district nurse appears, her dark blue coat fastened tight around her. I have seen her before at Grandma's house. Grandma calls her Laura.

"What's happened in there?" shouts one of the ladies outside the house.

The man looks over to the crowd, but doesn't answer. As I am so near the front, I can hear him grunt as he turns to the district nurse.

"Nurse, I think she's been gone for several days. I'll send for the undertaker if you will get her laid out."

"But, Dr Banks, how are we going to get her out?" she asks, pointing to the narrow dark stairs.

"Not my problem, Nurse," he says. "I'll send you the death certificate."

He walks to his car and is gone. The district nurse looks fierce.

"Go on!" she says to us all. "Show some respect."

She shuts Mrs Allsop's front door.

In the Co-op everyone is buzzing. There's a bit of cheer in the air and for once no one is crying.

"Turns out," says Mrs Wainwright, an older lady who lives almost across the road from Grandma, and who sells lovely apples, one penny for three, when her tree has some ready to eat, "Mrs Allsop's been dead for some days. Her son only noticed something was wrong when she stopped drinking the cups of tea and pieces of dry bread he'd been taking her. She hadn't come down the stairs for a few weeks and Mrs Stone tried to take her some hot food, but he wouldn't let her in."

Mrs Wainwright stops talking and looks around and about her. "Now," she whispers so we all have to lean in, "I've heard that Mrs Allsop is too large to bring down the stairs."

There is a big gasp from the shoppers. Someone says, "I know I shouldn't laugh but . . ."

"How are they going to get her out?" asks Rollie, who used to roll the cricket pitch and always talks to Father when we visit the recreation ground.

No one knows.

For once Mother isn't grumbling about how light our bag is, how little we have to eat.

"Hasn't had much of a life, that poor woman," she is saying, though I don't think she is really talking to me. "Husband died in the first one, and that son of hers has been a problem. Now she can't even die in peace, everyone in the village gossiping . . ."

Back home I can't stop thinking about Mrs Allsop. What does she look like now she is dead? How did the nurse know she was dead? Will she have to be dead in her house for ever? If someone dies in the war, in

Germany, will they have to stay on the ground there for ever? I go to find Jack. But he has gone out.

When we've put the food away and I have played with Bob, I ask Mother if I can go up the road and see what's happened to Mrs Allsop. She says yes, with no fuss at all, and says I am to come back to tell her if they need any help.

I almost bump into the district nurse, who is hurrying across the road with a lady who is covered from head to foot in black. She is wearing a small black hat, with a black flower at its back, a long black skirt which shows beneath a big black coat, and she is carrying a black bag. The group of women standing in front of the house step back to give them space.

"She been dead long?" calls someone from the crowd.

"That's not for me to say," replies the district nurse as she and the lady disappear into the house.

"Who's the woman in the funny black hat?" I ask Mrs Broome, Mike's mother. She lost Mike's father down the pit and I wonder if he is still down there, how they got him out. "Will she help Mrs Allsop out so she get up to heaven?"

Mrs Broome looks at the house and shakes her head from side to side and sighs a lot.

"That's Mrs Stone, Dot. She will be helping Mrs Allsop get ready."

"You could say that, me duck," says a woman next to us. "She's laying her out for the undertaker."

All eyes look up at the window again; a murmur of prayer passes across, as all now think about what Mrs Stone is doing.

Mother arrives with Bob.

"Oh, *there* you are, Dot," she says loudly, as if she didn't know where I was. "I thought I'd better come and find you, you've been so long."

I hope she isn't going to make me go back home, but she seems happy to stop and talk to some of the women. I hear murmurs of "too fat" and "through the window" and "how did it come to this?" as a big black car draws up. A man, also dressed all in black, steps out of the car, walks to the front door and gives it a whacking great knock with his cane. The district nurse lets him in, scowling at the crowd as she slams the door shut.

"The funeral people are here," says Mother. "Dot, run back home and fetch Father. I think they are going to need him."

I run as fast as I can all the way home, without stopping once, and call for Father. He is lying on the settee, but he's awake.

"Father!" I yell. "Come quick. Mother says you have to come to Mrs Allsop's house. She is stuck in her room and she's dead but can't get to heaven."

"Right you are, Dot," he says cheerily. "I'll come right away. Run back and tell your mother I will be along."

I run back. More people have arrived to look at what's going on. To my great surprise, a few minutes later, Father goes to Mrs Allsop's front door and knocks on it three times. The funeral man opens the window above.

"What is it?" he asks. He sounds sharp and cross.

"Excuse me, sir," says Father, "I hear the good lady can't be carried down those narrow stairs. Might we then lower her from the window?"

The district nurse's face appears. She looks rather red and hot.

"Oh, thank goodness. Some real help. Come on up, Joe."

Mrs Broome puts her arm on Father's sleeve.

"Go on, Joe. Let's get her out and to her heavenly maker."

"I'll try, Rose," replies Father. "Wish your Gilbert were here now to help."

He turns to Mrs Smallman, whose husband works down the mine with Father. "Bessie, can you go and ask your Fred if he can come up — we might need some help. And can you drop into Bill? I know he's on nights, but tell him we will need some muscle here pretty soon."

Jack's voice close to my ear makes me jump. He is with Bert and Arthur.

"What's happening? We went home for food and there's no one there. Where is everyone?"

It is my turn to know the answers. I puff myself up to deliver the news.

"Mrs Allsop has died, not in the war, in the house, and they can't get her to come out down the stairs. The district nurse and the man who came in the black car are upstairs, and they have asked Father to help them. Look up there."

"Can we go up?" asks Bert.

His answer comes but not from me. A bicycle bell rings.

"Move over, move over, move over, please," says Constable White as he circles the pavement.

"What took you so long, Constable?" asks one of the women. Constable White is always late when things happen in the village.

"Heard there was something happening at the top of the village, thought I'd better investigate." He knocks on the door, is let in, we hear shouting and almost at once, he comes out again.

"Ladies, and, hum, gentlemen," he says. "Have some respect for the lady lying upstairs, please. Will you all move back to the other side of the road? You're causing an obstruction."

In disorder we all move over to the other side of the road. When the Co-op van stops in the road, blocking everyone's view of the house, there is an outcry and Constable White goes over to ask the driver to move on.

Father's friends from the mine arrive. They have come up from the direction of the pit. Wound around their bodies they carry strong-looking lengths of rope. Two other miners are holding planks of wood and other things they have got from the pit. Mrs Allsop is nearer to heaven now.

The window slides open and Father appears. He takes out the glass and passes it behind him. Two of the miners stay in the street, holding up poles, and the other two go upstairs. Father shouts out things for people to do and a large white thing appears in the window. There is silence in the crowd and I know then

60

that I am about to see someone who is going to heaven. The few men in the crowd remove their hats. Rollie pokes Jack in the back and lifts his cap with his walking stick. Slowly the white mass moves forward.

"Look what they've got her on! It's her wardrobe door," shouts Aunt Betty, who has arrived just in time to see Mrs Allsop leave this world.

The white-wrapped mass continues to advance. "They've used her washing line to tie her on," says Mrs Broome.

The wardrobe door tips sideways. The two ladies beside me cover their eyes.

"Maybe she wants to get up," I whisper.

"Be quiet, Dot," Jack hisses. "She's dead."

The district nurse's arm slides out of one side of the window, and the lady who had come to get her ready appears at the other side. Mrs Allsop fills the whole window.

The wardrobe door is lowered from the window and the arms of the pole-holders push up hard. Now I can see Father. He is just inside the window and he is pulling on a rope. Fred is pulling on another rope behind him. One of the miners runs out of the door and heads towards Mrs Allsop. The wardrobe starts to turn.

"Let it down, let it down," calls Father. I wave up to him but he doesn't see me.

"Right you are, Joe," shouts one the pole-holders. "We're on an even keel now."

Mrs Allsop starts to come down over the front of her own house. Someone begins to say the Lord's Prayer, and with bowed heads we join them.

Some of the women start crying, moving over to wrap their arms around each other, and I remember the boy at school whose father has just died in the war. I will pray for Uncle Jim and all the other men from our village who have gone to the war and hope they don't die. Who will be there to help them if they die? The miners can't be there to help everyone.

And as we pray, I watch Mrs Allsop being lowered on the ropes until the miners down on the pavement grasp the door and place it on a waiting trolley.

I bury my head in Aunt Betty's skirt and start to cry.

There is much talk in the village about Mrs Allsop being lowered out of the window and Father and the miners are heroes. But Father brushes it off. He is worried about the news of bombed aeroplanes and ships being lost, and young men dying.

When Mrs Allsop's funeral is held at the Church of England at the Falling Ends, I hear Mother tell Father that a lot more people went than expected.

"Aye," says Father, "I expect they took the opportunity to go and have a chat with God."

CHAPTER
FOUR

A call for help

April 1941

For ages now I've been wearing my coat for more of the day than not. At school, my teacher Miss Mallory makes us wear our coats in class because the heating pipes have not been working and it is too cold to do lessons without them. One morning she has a bit of a fight with the caretaker over the pipes, when he says he can't warm them as he has no coal to heat the water.

"Well, Mr Blunt. My children are freezing and how can they learn, being so cold all day?" she says, as bravely as she can. "And besides, there's lots of coal just down the road at the mine. Can't you get some extra from there?"

No one stands up to the caretaker, so we all watch in silence, some of us forgetting to breathe.

"There's a war on, Miss Mallory." His voice is hard. "We get our rations, same as anyone else. We used all our coal up in the cold weather. Not my fault it's stayed so cold and wet. Perhaps you shouldn't be wasting your time teaching these children and go and do something useful to help your country!"

Miss Mallory turns to the blackboard and makes a few sniffing noises. It never works, trying to get something from the caretaker. He's the most frightening man I know. Father has said that even Hitler would surrender in the face of Mr Blunt.

I put up my hand. "Please, miss. My father works at the pit. Should I ask him if he can get us some coal?"

"My dad works there too," says Frances.

"Mine too!" shouts Eric. His father helped bring Mrs Allsop down through her window.

Miss Mallory holds up her hands.

"No, children, no. Mr Blunt would need a good deal of coal and we would get into an awful mess if you all tried to bring a little. Thank you for trying to help, but I think we will manage."

Mr Blunt gives us all a sour look and leaves.

Later in the playground, Eric, who is a long, thin, bony boy with his hands pulled up inside his coat sleeves, stands with a group of us in the playground. We decide to ask our fathers if they can get us some coal, whatever Miss Mallory has said, and make plans to bring it in a wheelbarrow to school.

Outside we have to wear our coats too as it hasn't stopped raining for days. It is so wet.

The village has changed. When it rains the Sheffield Road seems to shine and now that all the cobblestones have gone, the road is covered with something black. It has a very strong smell.

Jack bursts into the kitchen.

"Mother! Bert's got some of that black stuff on his shoes. George says it will burn his shoes off his feet and —"

Mother, who is filling the kettle, stops him speaking.

"Stop talking nonsense, Jack! It's tarmac. It won't burn his shoes, but it will certainly stick to them and they will be impossible to clean. Don't you go getting it on you."

"What have they put it down for?" I ask.

"Father says that it's better for car tyres, doesn't wear them out as fast as cobblestones do," says Mother. "Now we have the military camp and all their soldiers coming and going, we need to make sure our roads can take their lorries driving up and down all day."

I make a note never to walk on the tarmac. I only have one pair of shoes. Soon it will be the Easter holidays and I will be singing in the Sunday school anniversary service. I am getting worried that I don't have anything to wear as my summer frocks don't fit me any more and I don't have one for the cold and rain. After tea I try them on. The yellow one gets stuck and Mother nearly pulls my ears off as she tries to yank it over my head.

"What to do?" Mother says to Father. "I've no coupons to buy Dot a dress. Can you ask Flo if she has any spare material or scraps from one of her dresses?"

Aunt Flo's dresses are known around the village. She always looks what Mother calls "stylish". I am not sure if that is good or not, as Mother makes it sound a bit fishy. I think she looks lovely — pretty and like a princess. Before the war she used to give me shiny bits

65

of material for my dolls. Hope isn't the best dressed doll I've ever had as she arrived after the war started, but she still has her warm woollen dress.

Father agrees I should have something nice to wear, as this is my first year on the special platform that is put up for the service. Last year I was too little for it. This year I get to sing from the first rung. Next year on the next one up and up and up, until I am too old for the platform. Before the concert we go around the village green, singing to those who don't come to Chapel. We don't have a collection, but Mr Compton says that it is important to go so that we can take the Lord to those who don't come to his house. This year we have practised "Fight the Good Fight" and "There is a Green Hill Far Away".

"We must pray for and sing for all our loved ones who are fighting in other lands," says Mr Compton before, during and after each practice. Each time we respond with an "amen".

Tonight is our last practice. Maybe I will have to sing with my coat on. There are only two days to the concert and, while I know we all have to go without for the war, I pray that Father has let Mother use Aunt Flo's material. Last night I heard them talking while I was in the kitchen getting a glass of water.

"Where did that material come from, Nellie?" Father asked. "Did you get it in the market?"

"No, Joe. Your mother brought it up."

"And where did she get it from?"

Mother didn't reply.

"Come on, Nellie," said Father. "It's like dragging blood from a stone."

"She said she found it in one of your Flo's drawers," sighed Mother.

"And how did *she* get it?" Father pressed on.

"I've no idea, Joe. You know your Flo. Always manages to find a bargain, buys things when she sees them. It might have been lying there for years."

"Well, I hope your daughter doesn't get arrested on the Sunday school platform," snapped Father, and as I heard him come through the curtain, I ran up the stairs to bed.

I don't want to get arrested, whatever that is, and I don't want to think about Aunt Flo being up to something. She told Jack that she's planning to go into the army for women and I don't want her to get killed fighting.

Now, as I peep into the houseplace, I let all my breath out. There is white material, with little blue flowers on it, all over the table. There is tissue paper everywhere and a packet with a picture of a pretty girl standing with her arms held out. Mother has pins in her mouth and as she removes them, she puts them in a tin, carefully, one by one. When she can speak, she tells me to look after Bob, then she starts up the sewing machine.

"Put some milk on, Dot, and make him some Ovaltine while I try to get this finished. And keep him busy. He's been trying to get hold of the pins all afternoon."

Bob's face is all blotchy. He holds his arms out towards me and says, "Dodo, play giddy-up with me?" I take him into the kitchen and listen to the wonderful sound of the sewing machine. After he has his drink, I take him outside to play in the garden, doing up his little coat and ramming a hat over his golden curls. I will do anything Mother wants if it means I will have something to wear.

After Bob has had enough, we come inside. Mother says it is time for a fitting. I stand in my knickers and vest, waiting for the paper-covered pieces of material to be pinned around me. "Goodness knows if I will get this ready in time, what with all there is to do," Mother mumbles as she removes the unmade frock, pricking me with pins.

I make a deal with myself. I will sing extra-specially nicely in the Chapel tonight to see if God can hear me and make the sewing machine work well. I will also pray for everyone in the village who has gone off to war to come home safely. I will look after Bob as much as Mother wants and do all my chores without any fuss. And I will keep my fingers crossed for the whole rehearsal.

I get to the Chapel early and go through to look for June. But when I hear crying coming from the top of the chancery, I creep in to see what's to do.

"I don't think we should do it. I don't think I can do it," sobs Mrs Boroughs, the kind lady who let us into her house to hear our carols last Christmas. She is a very good organist and plays in our Chapel at the special services.

She has her head on her husband's shoulder. His face is turned towards me and I think he is going to cry too. For a moment the two of them stand holding each other. Then with a choking sound Mr Boroughs says: "You see, Compton, with all this going on —" he waves one arm in the air "— we wonder if we should hold the anniversary at all."

Mr Compton raises his hands, but says nothing. Aunt Lily is standing next to him. I crouch down even further.

"Mr Boroughs, when I heard your news I can't tell you how sad it made me . . ." Aunt Lily's voice sounds soft, different to any way I have heard her talk before. "All we can do is hope that he bailed out in time. They haven't said that he didn't."

"That's just clutching at straws," manages Mrs Boroughs, between sobs.

"If you really feel that we should cancel, then we must consider it," says Aunt Lily, turning to Mr Compton.

"No!" I whisper, maybe a bit too loudly. This is my first year of singing on the platform. I've waited all my Chapel-life for this. I lie flat on the floor, but Mr Compton has heard me. He pulls me up and, grasping my hand, swings me to the front of the Chapel. Aunt Lily gasps.

"Arthur," he says, hurting me as he holds me too tight. "Your news has made me sadder than I can say, but this child has practised for weeks so that she can sing to Jesus. Sing and ask him for his help and comfort, care for all of us. He listens to children and we should let them sing his praise."

Mrs Boroughs puts her hand on my head. She looks up to the top of the altar, to me, to the statue of Jesus and back to me. "Yes. Yes. I do believe you are right, Mr Compton. It's what Charles would want, Arthur. But we need to keep it quiet. I couldn't bear everyone looking at me, knowing that Charles is missing in action."

I feel like crying. I can see Charles's face and the beautiful girl who held his arm when we were singing carols. Why do the Germans want to make us all so unhappy? What have we done to make them so cross with us all the way over here?

As people start to come into the chapel, Mrs Boroughs wipes her eyes and goes over to the organ. "Thank you, Dot," says Aunt Lily, her voice halfway between soft and hard. "Now, go into the schoolroom and tell the other children we are ready for them."

Our places on the rising platform have already been arranged. This year I am to sit four steps up from the bottom. June sits beside me, George three steps above and his older brother Harry only two rows from the top. We clamber to our positions and sit in silence, each of us knowing that the "wrath of God" would look like nothing compared to our parents' wrath if we were sent home for misbehaving.

Mother spends all of Saturday finishing my dress. Grandma Compton comes over with some blue buttons she found in a tin. My dress, with its gathered skirt, small puffed sleeves, blue flowers that Grandma calls forget-me-nots, makes me feel like a princess. Grandma tells Mother more about the missing airman and Mrs Boroughs waiting in all day for telegrams, sending Mr Boroughs out to the Post Office on the hour, every hour to see if any news has arrived. No sooner does he return home than he has to go back out again.

Now, after my bath-in-honour-of-the-Easter-concert, the real pain of looking pretty begins. My hair is to be done so I look like Mother's favourite, Shirley Temple. This means I have to have ringlets instead of plaits. I wish I had Bob's fair curls that spring up all around his head, but instead my hair hangs down straight.

Father has gone for a whistle-wetter "to wash the coal dust out". He says this every week, to which Mother always replies "must be some dust down that pit, Joe". But she smiles at him as he leaves. After she has put Bob to bed, I sit in my nightdress on the peg rug and lean back against her knees. On the settee beside her are lots of thin strips of material, torn from an old pillowcase. Mother calls them the rags.

Mother takes a rag, places it across my head and hangs it down over my face. I take hold of it. She combs a thin strip of hair and wraps it around and around the bottom half of the rag, I hang onto the other end. When the strip of hair has been wound, I pass Mother the other end of the rag and she winds it around the wet curl and ties the two ends of the rag together somewhere by my neck. I can't move until all my hair and all the strips have been used. Mother has a very strong pull and sometimes the pain makes my eyes water.

"If you want to look beautiful, Dottie, you sometimes have to suffer pain. Well, at least women suffer pain. When I was younger, we used to wear pretty dresses and during the Great War you couldn't get stockings so we used to shave our legs with our fathers' old razors, which left our legs in ribbons. Then we'd splosh methylated spirit all over them to stop the bleeding. You don't know how easy you have it these days, my girl."

In the morning I am amazed that I have slept at all. All the lumps and bumps in my head made it hard to get comfortable. At breakfast Jack can hardly eat for laughing at the sight of me. Father takes him into the kitchen and Jack returns with his lips pressed tightly together and he doesn't look at me.

Before the proper concert, the choir are to go around the green, singing to the village. For this my curling rags are to stay in my hair and I am to wear my normal clothes. My new dress is hanging on the door, waiting for later. I pull a woollen winter hat over my rags and walk up to the Chapel. I see Aunt Lily on the way, her metal curlers sticking out from under a large cotton headscarf. Lots of the other ladies have the same curlers and June's rags are jammed under a large straw hat.

I hear Aunt Betty talking to a lady. "Mrs Boroughs won't be with us this morning. She's saving herself for the service."

I remember what Grandma Compton said to Mother and think she must be waiting at home for a telegram to arrive, just in case her son has been found.

The Chapel door crashes open and the small pedal organ comes hurtling out, Mr Compton shouting instructions. Mr Boroughs is in charge of pushing it on its two front wheels and we all set off after it, hurrying along to keep up. The organ comes to a halt just after the Co-op and in front of the pub. Mr Compton hands out some sheets of music and we gather round. Mrs Compton, a large, red-faced woman, works away madly on the foot pedal and the organ begins to make some strange noises. After a few coughs the organ produces musical notes and we start to sing. There is no collection. We are singing for Jesus. I add Mrs Borough's son to my list of people I need to sing for.

We travel slowly down Sheffield Road, the organ rocking and bumping across to where it meets the Top Road. Here we stop and sing again. Then we wind our way up Top Road to the Post Office and some of the ladies complain of the cold and a large black cloud makes it go dark. As we go down School Road, the first spot of rain falls. But we sing on, to the people who have come out of their houses to listen.

Happy from the success of those songs, Mr Compton says we will go further on down the hill past the church. He likes to think we are better singers than the church choir. But Aunt Lily feels differently.

"I'm not standing out in the rain," she says. "I've spent all night with these in." She touches the curler that sticks out of her scarf. "I'm not having my hair ruined before I get my curlers out."

It seems that most of the ladies agree and so the organ is pushed back to the Chapel, Mr Compton making us sing as we walk back.

On the way back, I peel off to my house, telling Aunt Flo that I am away. Mother makes me hurry my dinner and then removes the rags. Ringlets hang around my face. Mother pushes her finger up each one and brushes it smooth. Bob gets quite excited by them.

"Dodo. I pull, pull," he shouts, and reaches over to pull my hair. I don't mind but Mother is not happy and slaps his fingers, telling him he has made one ringlet longer than the rest. While I was out this morning, Mother starched my dress and now as I put it on it stands out around my legs. I feel like one of the ballet dancers I have seen in a film at the picture house. The blue ribbon, which Aunt Mabel had found for me, sits high on my head and holds the ringlets back from my face. I feel stiff and I hardly dare move, but for one moment I feel excited and pleased with myself.

Mother lifts and drops the dress and puts my ringlets in place.

"You look lovely," she says as she kisses my cheek. "Come on. I'm going to take you to that Chapel for once."

And so it is that I walk up the road holding Father's hand on one side and Mother's on the other. As we cross the Sheffield Road, there is a feeling of excitement in the air and you can tell everyone is dressed in their finest, so many feathers dancing on Sunday-best hats.

When we get to the gates of the Chapel, Mother tells me to sing well and be a good girl. And then she turns and is gone. Father takes me into the schoolroom where we children are always sent, always waiting, out of the way. A boy who I saw at one of the practices shoots out of the kitchen door. He wears a large tie over a shirt that looks too big for him. I take off my coat so he can see my dress, but he has gone.

I find June and look at her dress and she looks at mine and we look at the other girls without letting them see we are looking, and we decide our dresses are the nicest. As the big organ sounds I think of Mrs Boroughs and her missing son and hold my head up. I will pray for them and I will sing for them. Without looking left or right, following the girl in front, I climb the three steps, turn and sit. Straightening out my dress I look across the Chapel. I can see Mike, his beautiful voice at the ready, standing at the front. I can see Father and Jack and Bob and Grandma and Grandfather and all my aunts and uncles, apart from Uncle Jim. I sit on my hands so I don't wave. I bob my head so my curls dance.

We all sing along with the congregation, and then the choir sings with us. I have learnt all the words and feel like I'm singing from inside my heart.

Mr Boroughs stands up to talk to the congregation. There is silence and nobody moves.

"We must remember," he says, his voice strong and wobbly at the same time, "all those who cannot be with us today and all who will in future be called to war."

There is a mumbling of amen and then Mike sings the first verse of "The Lord is My Shepherd" all by himself. There is some crying from the congregation and some of the ladies miss their entry when the organ brings us in to finish the hymn.

After the concert, we children are all given a carrot on a stick as a treat for our "angelic singing". Back home I don't want to take my dress off and Mother lets me keep it on until bedtime. The next time I wear it is to sing at a special service for Frank Boroughs. A few weeks after the Easter service, Mr Boroughs stopped going to the Post Office seven times a day. Frank's body was found in a field in France. Mrs Boroughs never played the organ again.

CHAPTER
FIVE

A day that ends with a bang

August 1942

The sun shines as I shout goodbye to June. It is warm — sunny and bright — and I have just had my last day in the infants. I am seven years old; when I go back to school after the summer holidays, I will be in Junior Girls. As I dance up the Sheffield Road, I think of all the soldiers that passed through in a convoy on their way to fight a few weeks ago and hope that they will all come back before school starts up again. Especially Bert and Arthur's father.

We are supposed to be meeting up at the traffic lights when the boys finish school, but as soon as I throw open the kitchen door and see Mother standing by the dolly tub, her face red and her mood dark, I get a feeling I won't be going anywhere.

"Oh, there you are, Dorothy. Roll your sleeves up and help me."

My balloon of happiness pops. Mother is washing the enormous blanket from her bed and it will take ages to get it through the mangle.

"Hold it off the floor while I mangle it." She lifts the blanket out of the water and feeds it through the rollers. As it comes through I catch it. It's not too bad at first, but after a while the whole thing comes through and is heavy and wet in my arms. The feeling of wet wool makes me shudder. Mother wipes her hands and in a tunnel of blanket we head through the houseplace and into the garden. A white blanket from the boys' bed and my pink one are hanging on the line. Huffing and puffing, she hurls her end over the line. I let my side go and my arms feel like thunder.

"That will do for today, Dorothy," sighs Mother. "We'll do one another day, if it stays sunny."

Aunt Lily is hanging up her washing too. She puts her head over the fence that lies between the yards.

"Have you heard, Nellie?" she asks. "They say there's been a bombing in Chesterfield. In broad daylight."

"It's getting a bit too close, isn't it?" says Mother as she adjusts the prop under the washing line, narrowly missing Father's newly planted cabbages. I know she is worried about the bombs in the city. When Father went on the bus to his Miners' Union meeting last week she was in a state in case he got bombed.

As Mother and Aunt Lily talk more about bombs and the war and how worried Bert and Arthur's mother is about her husband, I slip away. Bob is at Grandma Compton's and so I call to Mother that I am going to fetch him.

Jack, Mike, Harry and George are at the traffic lights. The lights were recently brought to our village because there is now so much coming and going from the military camp that without them the traffic kept getting into a muddle. It has taken us a while to work out how they change colour, but now, if we all jump at the same time onto the black rubber pads that lie in the road, we can get the traffic light to go from red to orange to green. After changing the colours a few times, we call for Bert and Arthur and head for the recreation ground. We stop by to look at the newly installed siren. A few weeks ago two men put a large pole in the ground by the paper shop. They climbed the pole and put a green box at its top. Father told us that the box was a siren that would sound if any German planes were coming to drop bombs on us. It worked because three nights after it arrived it went off and all the people in the village heard it and got to a shelter in time. It had nearly shaken us out of bed and we'd gone downstairs, into the pantry, which is off the kitchen, and had finished the night on, and under, the stone benches under the stairs. Wrapped in a blanket I had stood in Mother's dolly tub among the clothes as if I was waiting to be washed. Father had been grim-faced. "Looks like they might be with us in the next few weeks," he'd said. But so far we had been safe.

We play Cowboys and Indians for the rest of the afternoon and it is only after I have been captured and tied to a tree that I remember Bob. It takes a lot of persuasion to get Harry to untie me.

On the morning of the first day of the school holidays Mother is not about to let us sit around.

"Grandma came up to see me last night," she tells us. "She wants you to go and see her this morning, straight after breakfast. Eat up and off you go. Take Bob with you. Maybe you can be as useful as your big brother." Jack has already left. He is helping on the farm, getting ready for the harvest. Sometimes he comes home with a few extra potatoes for us and he is pleased with himself when there is more food on our table.

Grandma is waiting for us. "Oh, I'm glad to see you two. I don't know what I'm going to do about them."

She hands us each an empty jam jar. Her front garden is no longer awash with colour but is green and white, cabbages and cauliflowers popping up from the ground.

"Look," she says, pointing at the leaves. "They're all covered in caterpillars, the cabbage white butterflies won't leave them alone. They're eating all the leaves. At this rate we'll have nothing left for the winter. Can you two pick them all off?"

Grandma Compton is so kind to us and makes us lovely things to eat and Father says she is getting old and is very upset about the war, especially now Aunt Flo has gone off to be in the Ladies Army. I think it would be unkind to say no, even though I don't much care for creepy-crawlies. So Bob and I spend a back-aching morning filling our jars with green caterpillars. Every so often I stop to see if Bert and Arthur, who live next door to Grandma, are anywhere to be seen, but they must have gone to the farm with Jack. Their garden is full of potato plants, and beans growing up a trellis where a beautiful blue flower used to grow.

We collect as many caterpillars as we can. Bob is slower than me as he likes them to crawl up and down his arms. Grandma says that Grandfather Compton will do something with them later. We have a drink and a piece of cake as a reward, but as we are getting ready to leave Grandma says she hasn't finished with me.

"Dorothy, you know how to knit, don't you? Now you are on school holidays, you can make yourself useful and join our Thursday-night knitting group."

As she speaks she is undoing a small yellow jumper, winding the wool into a skein around the back of a high-backed wooden chair.

"We're knitting scarves and gloves to take down to the soldiers in the camp. Come the winter, if this wretched war is still on, they might have to go to some very cold places."

I wanted to have as much free time in the holidays as possible but the knitting group will be a good place to sit quietly and listen to the gossip and what's really going on. I could knit Mr Baker a scarf and make sure the twins send it to him. It is bad enough thinking of him being shot at, but being cold as well could be too much. I tell Grandma that I will come on Thursday but daren't risk gloves, as I'm not that good a knitter and the soldiers might need five fingers to shoot a gun and I don't think I can guarantee gloves with five fingers.

The rest of the week is busy. Once Grandma tells her friends and neighbours how good Bob and I are at collecting pesky caterpillars, we are asked to help them out too. It's a good week for extra pieces of cake and dodging housework with Mother, and my knitting gets off to a good start. I sit in the corner, listening as I knit, and hear all about Mrs Mackenzie's daughter's new boyfriend from the military camp and how he got into trouble for leaving the camp to sneak out and see her.

With all this work, I am glad when Annual Week arrives. This is Father's holiday from the pit and we are allowed to stop working too. Before the war he had a whole week off, but now that so many of the men in our village are in the war, he only has four days. Thankfully he is off for the Annual Sports Day, the best day in our village all year, the recreation ground buzzing with noise and excitement. In Chapel, the Sunday before, we pray for all the men who can't be there to take part and, just before the amen, for a lovely sunny day. It has been raining on and off and Father keeps having to go back to mark out the lines for the races. He and Rollie are in charge of that.

Bob and I are taking part in the children's fancy-dress parade and will dress up, after the races, as Jack and Jill. We practised last week. Bob is going to be Jill and I am going to be Jack. Jack is not going to be anyone. We will carry Mother's white enamel pail between us. Bob will wear one of my old dresses and a baby bonnet and Father has made him some plaits from string he found in the cupboard. I will put on a pair of Jack's old trousers and a jumper and push my plaits under one of Jack's old caps.

We walk with Mother up the Sheffield Road and it seems that everyone left in the village is heading towards the Sports Day. It's noisy and cheery and bright, as if this was before and there isn't a war on. The entrance to the lane that leads to the ground is too narrow for everyone at the same time and a large crowd is waiting to get into the competition. A group of boys from Crich Road run down Top Road, ahead of their mothers and sisters. The lure of earning a few pennies in the races is making them practise their running. Their metal-soled boots ring loud on the pavement pebbles. Mother watches them. "They look a bit more lively now than they did before the war. At least rationing helps them get some food."

Father and Jack left early to help set things up and I look around to see if I can spot them. First, I want to explore the stalls. There are signs over the stalls: "BUY A SPITFIRE," "PENNY A GO". The rain we had a week or so ago has made the grass green and the buttery sun is warm and inviting. I go with Mother and Bob to her favourite, the bran tub. With fierce concentration she throws the dart at a number board, a packet of Woodbines at stake. When she doesn't win, she asks for another go and tells me sharply to "go and find your brother and take Bob with you".

I see Jack, Bert and Arthur at the "Splat the Rat" stall. If you're fast enough to knock the rolled-up socks as they shoot out of a piece of drainpipe, you can win one penny, which I think you are expected to put in the Spitfire Fund tin. Arthur and Jack win fourpence each, which now clicks its way into the tin, though I see them keeping back a penny each. We move over to a new stall that the man tells us is all about knocking Hitler and his henchmen over with wooden balls. There's nothing to win but the pleasure of doing it. There is a great big queue for this one but we wait in line until it is our turn. Between us, Bob and I knock them all down. Arthur says to Bert that if he can knock all the henchmen down this will mean their father will come home. We leave them knocking down Hitler, a grim concentration on Bert's face.

I run along by the sports field. The big swings are crowded, some of the boys jumping when the swing is highest. I see Bob, his arms held out sideways, zooming around the field, knocking down the boys who are pretending to be German planes. I see June with her father and wave. She is wearing pale yellow shorts, a clean white blouse and bright white plimsolls. I look down at my scruffy old dress and my scuffed-up school shoes.

I head away from the crowds and towards the far end of the field, towards a group of men sitting together. Each man is wearing a coloured scarf in the neck of his shirt. As I walk past, one of them looks up at me, his face scarred blue.

"Hello, me duck," he says. "And which face are you planning to pull for?"

"My father put a blue scarf on this morning so I think I'd better pull for them," I answer. The miners have a tug of war each Sports Day and the men who work on each of the pit's coalfaces pull against each other. It's a knockout competition and the last standing pull against the pit management.

"Who's he then, lass?" he asks.

"Joe Compton," I say with pride.

"Hey, this is Joe's lass," he tells the other. "Well, bugger me, who'd have thought he could make a pretty lass!"

Just as I feel myself go red, a voice sounds out from a megaphone. I run as fast as I can to the stalls and squeeze my way to the front of the crowd.

"Ladies and gentlemen . . ." A variety of calls ring out in answer to this. He tries again. "Ladies and gentlemen, the races are about to begin, but before the proceedings can start would you please give a rousing welcome to Mr Jackson, the under-manager at Brompton Colliery." I hear the men behind me, whistling and cheering — and booing, in what sounds like a friendly way.

"Thank you, thank you. Ladies and gentlemen, the Brompton Colliery Management are pleased to have sponsored the prizes for today's winners and to be donating substantially to Rompton's efforts towards buying a Spitfire."

There is polite clapping from the crowd, interrupted by shushing as the vicar from the church at the Falling Ends takes the megaphone.

"Ladies and gentlemen, before we start our races, please join me in saying a prayer for those who have gone away and will not be coming back to us, and for those who still fight to bring us peace."

"Speak up!" shouts someone from behind me.

He holds his hands together above his head and people soon see what is going on. Hands held above our heads, heads bowed, we come together to say the Lord's Prayer. The amens ring out for some time and the prayer is said again. The lady next to me can't manage the prayer a second time.

"Is she all right?" asks a woman who stands beside us.

"She's got two sons and a daughter fighting and two down the pit," replies another.

The man who was first to speak takes the megaphone back. "Thank you for showing your respect, ladies and gentlemen. If I can just have your attention a moment or two longer, please welcome two guests to whom I think we should say an enormous thank you. Two heroes from our village, who have fought valiantly in the name of our great country." Pushed from behind by helping hands, two young men in khaki uniform limp onto the field. The crowd cheers and claps for a very long time and the two men go bright red in the face.

"And now," says the man with the megaphone, "the bit you have all been waiting for. The races." And with that begins the fun.

I go over and watch the small children's races. Miraculously, Bob wins the small children's egg and spoon race. He seems to have a very large spoon and, once again, I think his blond curls and blue eyes have helped him get the biggest spoon.

"Girls seven years to ten years, please come to the line," says the announcer, and I run to the starting line.

This is the first year I have been with this age group and they all look so big. The girl next to me, who I don't recognise, wears some very large pink knickers over her dress and no shoes. A man shouts, "On your marks, get set . . . go!" From that moment I only see the back of pink knickers. It is the first time that I have not won the fifty-yards dash. Maybe I'll have to wait a year or so until I grow. Still, I come a "valiant" second, which makes Mother smile and Aunt Betty jump up and down with excitement, though she might have been just jumping up and down anyway.

I watch all the boys' races. Jack and Arthur win the three-legged race. Bert and I enter the mixed children's three-legged, but he falls down before we even set off from the starting line.

And then it is time for the tug of war, the event for which the whole village stops what it's doing and comes together. Jack proudly helps Father and Uncle Arthur pull the thick ropes across the field while we all settle down to watch. As the miners get into their teams, we shout and cheer, but when the first team captains shake hands, silence falls. In work vests and trousers along with pit boots they begin the tug.

Father pulls for the blue team and soon just the blue team and the red team remain from the six starters. The pull is equal. I can see Father's boots digging into the earth and moving backwards, but then the anchorman slips and forward they go. We cheer and whistle and clap and shout. It is a long pull, but suddenly, and I am not sure why, the blues are over the line.

There is a loud cheer as the reds hold up their hands. Now the managers, mostly dressed in cricket whites, step onto the field. They spend a good deal of time preparing themselves, but eventually they take the rope and the referee calls, "Pull." As easy as a walk across a meadow, the managers are pulled forward. A couple of miners get grass marks on their knees, but the rest hardly dirty their boots. It's over. In one tug.

We just have time to run home and get changed for the fancy dress. We stand behind Old Mother Hubbard and a Spitfire and wait our turn to walk in front of the judges. We don't win, but when Bob pulls off his bonnet and string plaits, one of the judges asks, "Are you a boy?"

Bob goes red.

"Then you are a girl, are you?" She looks down on me. "Oh, that is quite wonderful! I think you should get a special prize."

She gives threepence directly to Bob. "Such a pretty face, such pretty hair. I was sure you were a little girl."

After the prize-giving, the under-manager stands on a wooden box, the knees of his trousers grass-stained. "Ladies and gentlemen," he says, "thank you for coming to the Miners' Recreation Sports Day. We have raised a good deal of money for the Spitfire Fund and we shall put the final amount up on the village noticeboard. We shall resume donating to the National Savings Group at Rompton Infants. We hope you have had a memorable day. Keep up your good work for our boys abroad and our boys here, at home, keeping the coal fires burning."

There is some scuffling and a man's voice, which takes some time to get going, sings: "Pack up your troubles in your old kit bag . . ." We all sing with him, and as we think of the enemy, who sit on the other side of the English Channel, we join in with "The White Cliffs of Dover". We end with "God Save the King" and three cheers for our boys.

On Monday we go back to school, so Mother says we have to get used to going to sleep earlier. But it's very hot and still light outside and I can't settle. I stand beside the half-open bedroom window and look out across the gardens into the gathering dusk. The sun has just disappeared behind the Crich Hills and in the red glow I can see people working in their gardens, tending to their growing food. Aunt Lily has turned out to have what Mother calls green fingers, her vegetable patch by far and away the most productive in our little row of houses. Potatoes and carrots are her speciality.

Jack is still out in the garden. Next week he turns ten. I watch as he helps Mother remove the dead flowers from her beloved tiger lilies. There are only a few left, a little reminder of better days, as Mother says. Father strolls down the garden path, the newspaper tucked under his arm. He's heading for the lavatory, where he will sit and have a last read of yesterday's paper before he rips it into small squares and hangs it on the string at the back of the lavatory door. It's nice watching everyone from up here and I look up to see if I can spot the aeroplane throbbing in the distance. More and more of them are crossing our skies nowadays, the noise constant during some parts of the day. Yesterday, as the planes went over Mother looked upwards and murmured, "Some poor creatures are going to have it tonight."

As I think about Mrs Borough's son falling out of his plane to the ground, the noise of the aeroplane overhead becomes deafening, as if it is actually in our garden. And then a boom, more than just a sound, shakes the bed. I throw my arms across my face and fall to the floor, spinning away from Mother and Father's bed. Dust and pieces of dirt fall over my face. The window rattles violently and the whole room seems to move.

I hear my father screaming. Pulling myself up, I look out the window. Through what looks like a cloud of dark mist, he stumbles forward, his trousers around his ankles making him fall.

"Nellie!" he yells. "I've been shot! I've been shot in the backside."

For a moment there is an unreal silence. The dark cloud has now crossed the gardens and pieces of earth fall from the sky. Mother runs down the garden path. But where is Jack? I must go to help her. I regain my senses and head for the stairs. Bob is sitting up in bed.

"Stay there!" I shout, but he jumps out of bed and I take hold of his chubby hand and together we go down the stairs. The air is filled with flying pieces of dirt and the houseplace floor is covered in what feels like grit.

Outside, there is shouting all across the gardens. There is a glow in the distance, red, blue and yellow. Mother and Jack are half-carrying Father along the garden path.

"What's happened"? I shout, running towards them.

"Get out here, you two," says Father, through gritted teeth. "We mustn't go back in the house until we get the all-clear."

"Jack," says Mother firmly, "go back inside as quick as you can and get a chair and cushion for your father."

"Why didn't they sound the siren?" asks Mrs Walker from over the fence. "We've had enough practices. Typical. When it happens for real they forget to sound the thing."

One of the ARP men comes through. Father is an ARP warden, his tin hat stationed on the mangle. But he's not going to be much use tonight in this state.

"Everyone all right here?" he asks, looking down our garden and over the fence. He catches sight of Father. "What's this, Joe? You been injured? I'd just come to tell you we need every man out."

"Sorry, Jim," says Father. "I was down the garden, something shot me in the back." He points to his backside. "Must be a bit of shrapnel," he mumbles.

"Can we go back in the house, Ernie?" asks Mother.

"Aye, Nellie. We think these houses are safe, but check your water and gas when you go in. If they've been ruptured in any house in the row, don't stay. Come straight up to the village hall and tell us."

Mother crunches her way through the houseplace, her hands to her face. Father attempts to follow with Jack's help and with a loud yelp, lowers himself back onto the seat of the chair. He looks like he has seen a ghost. Mother orders us up to bed. We don't argue, but

I lie in with Jack so he can tell me what he thinks has happened.

In the morning the garden is covered in grey dust and it looks dirty and sad. Mother is on her hands and knees washing the kitchen floor, hair hanging over her face. She is coughing badly and I think maybe she has been up all night sorting the house.

"Is Father all right?" I ask. He didn't come to bed last night.

"He'll live." She coughs some more. "I mightn't though. Now mind that wet floor and go and get Bob some breakfast. I am going to need your help today, after last night's to-do. First time a bomb has hit us, Dot. And hopefully the last."

We wipe and dust and polish all morning. Bob and Jack help too. But as soon as we think it's clean, the dust settles again and it takes ages to get the house back to what Mother calls "a fit and proper state".

As soon as we are able, Jack and I are out of the house, heading to the twins' house. As we come round the corner on to the Sheffield Road we see several groups of women chattering by the roadside.

"Can't go any further down the road," says Arthur importantly. He and Bert are sitting on the wall outside their house. Bert points to an army lorry and a group of soldiers who are examining the road.

"They are looking to see if there is an unexploded bomb," continues Arthur.

"Did it break your windows?" I ask, looking up at their bedroom.

"Yeah," says Bert. "Our bedroom window and the kitchen one. Our Mum doesn't know how to fix them, so the ARP man said he might be able to come back later and help us. Our father would have known what to do."

Bert looks as if he is about to cry. I will ask Father to help Mrs Baker when he is better. At that moment Mike comes running towards us.

"Have you heard?" he puffs. "The side of the infant school at the Falling Ends has been blown out."

"Blast!" says Jack. "Means us juniors will have to go back on Monday."

Grandma Compton, Aunt Betty and Mrs Broome come up the path to talk to Mrs Baker. I follow them into the house. Recently, I have come to realise that women do all the useful talking round here and if you want to know anything, it's best to sit quietly and listen.

Mrs Baker is in her usual armchair. She is a large woman and hasn't been able to do much since her husband left for the war. Aunt Betty makes everyone a cup of tea. When she hands them out she sees me sitting in the corner of the room.

"Dot!" she says. "I didn't see you there. Come and sit with me and I'll re-do your plaits."

I sit in front of her and she takes the bands out of my hair. Aunt Betty likes to make me look pretty. Mostly I try and dodge her, but today it might be useful.

"They dropped three bombs," says Mrs Baker. "Two landed in Yellow Yard just as Jimmy was putting a fire out."

"Did they get Mr Walker's pigeon huts?" Aunt Betty asks. Mr Walker keeps pigeons in Yellow Lane, right next to the yard.

"Yes," says Mrs Broome. "And that's what caused all this. You know the top of the pigeon huts are painted white, to help the pigeons find them? Well, they say the German bomber was looking for the Butterly Ironworks where they make those war tanks. Apparently he got confused because he was being chased by a British plane. I heard that the German pilot probably mistook the white roofs of the pigeon huts for the roof of the factory, panicked and dropped his bombs. Pfff!"

"Lucky no one got hurt," says Aunt Betty.

"Father did," I say.

"What?" says Grandma Compton in surprise. "Where? Is he all right? Come on, Dot. I need to see him. You can tell me what happened on the way home."

We walk back, Grandma pushing herself as fast as she can. Father is sitting in his armchair, two cushions beneath, puffing on his pipe and looking a bit sorry for himself.

"Joe! What happened?" says Grandma, collapsing onto the settee next to Mother. "Is it the shrapnel that's got you?"

"No, Mother, it's not the shrapnel. Laura came round to examine him. His buttock is black and blue with a great big blood blister running right across it. Never seen anything like it in all the time she's been nursing, she said. She and I went down to the lavatory, where it happened, and you'll never guess what . . ."

I sit quietly, trying to be invisible, before Mother decides I shouldn't hear.

"What, Nellie?" asks Grandma.

"Well," says Mother, "the lavatory seat is split right across. And we examined it and Laura thinks the seat, which Joe was sitting on, was split open by the explosion, and when the air was drawn back out the split was slammed closed. She said it was lucky it was his buttock that took it and not —"

She looks across at Grandma and notices me for the first time. She nods in the direction of Father's lap.

Father looks a bit sheepish, as though he would rather be in the pub, or down the pit, anywhere but here with us staring at him.

Grandma Compton gets up with a great sigh. "I know just the thing," she says. "I'll be back soon with one of my potions."

"That's all I need," grumbles Father. Grandma Compton's famous potions have a good effect on some people — like me, when I had a toothache — but Father runs a mile every time Grandma comes near him with one. "And I won't even be able to get off my backside to escape."

And so we survive the German bombing and life goes on in our village. Everyone is talking about the bombs and I am quiet and small wherever I go so that I can pick up more information. At the knitting group, I learn that three bombs dropped on the road to Rompton a short distance past the Falling Ends, and that miraculously they did little damage because, as I overheard one of the knitters say, the soft ground lessened the impact of the blasts. In the Co-op, as I wait in line, I hear that the main blast crossed School Road, taking out some shop windows, and travelled up the gardens behind the houses, landing with some force on our lavatory, and that most of the apple trees that grow in the orchard next to the school have disappeared. Mr Walker tells Father that his pigeon sheds look dishevelled but that they are still there. I don't hear what happened to the pigeons, but we know that they are used in the war, so we hope they managed to fly to safety. Father says we should all be proud that our good old Derbyshire stone was able to withstand German bombing.

Unfortunately, our school is not damaged as badly as we first thought. The wall facing the blast has rocked but not fallen, and a small part of the roof has been blown off. At Chapel, I hear a woman telling another that her husband said the wall had not gone down because it was only a single brick thick, saved by the council being such "mean buggers" and not building double walls.

Within a day or two of the blasts, there are men on the school roof, hammering tarpaper down across the hole; the windows that were broken now have wooden boards nailed across them. Life soon goes back to normal, but for one evening we hear our village mentioned on the wireless and Yellow Yard becomes famous.

Father returns to work at the end of his holiday. He is still in pain but he says he would sooner be down the pit than facing all the silly remarks that people in the village make. Back at school we have to draw a picture of what happened. I draw a picture of Father running up the garden path with the bomb behind him, an arrow pointing to his backside.

CHAPTER
SIX

Piggy-wiggy, boogie-woogie

December 1943

Something isn't quite right. Father sounds strange, like the sort of voice Jack uses when he is guilty of doing something naughty.

"You're still going through with it then, Joe?" Mother sighs.

"As far as I know. I've heard nothing to the contrary. Don't fret, Nellie. Nothing will go wrong. My father knows what he is doing."

And having pulled on his pit boots, cap and scarf, Father disappears out of the door, giving it a good bang behind him.

Mother does not look happy. She coughs for what seems like a long time. Ever since she went to hospital last year with pneumonia, she has frequent coughing fits.

"They could go to prison, the lot of them," she splutters as we clear the table. She clearly has something on her mind, so when Jack and I ask to go out into the snow, she doesn't say no. We dress as quickly as possible, taking care to wrap Bob up warm. We are going out to look for the Americans.

The military camp, just outside of the village, now has lots and lots of soldiers from America. They come into the village and walk around. At assembly, Mrs Meeks told us that they are our friends who have travelled a long way to help us fight the war. She said we must be cheerful and friendly, and that even though they are from the other side of the world, they speak English and we can talk to them when we see them. Jack told me that they come from the same place as the cowboy Roy Rogers, who we see in films at the picture house. At home, Father wasn't as happy about the Americans being here as Mrs Meeks is, but after three of them had come to tea and we had talked and played cricket, Father said he liked them. Mother is still talking about the tin of cling peaches they gave her — half the village came into the house to have a look at them — and has hidden away the other gift, a pair of nylon stockings that she is saving for the end of the war. Now, I look for Alvin, Elmer and Pete every time I go into the village, but I haven't seen them for a while. Maybe, says Father, they have gone away to fight.

Jack says he has seen Alvin and we are off to see if we can find him. After we have collected Bert and Arthur and Mike we head to the Falling Ends, a good starting point as it leads to several pubs. Father complains that the Americans are getting too fond of his beer and drinking up our rations.

"We'll ask them if we can sing songs for them," I suggest as I jog along, trying to keep up with the boys.

"Yeah," says Bert, trying to sound like an American. "We'll sing if they give us some gum to eat."

"You don't *eat* gum," says Jack, as if Bert is a dummy. "You just chew it."

Bert, who loves eating and is now puffing as we quicken our pace, stops, his breath short. Bob and I stop with him.

"Why would you chew it if you can't eat it?" he says, confused.

"You can ask them for a candy bar," suggests Bob, who is six now and bright as a button. "You can eat candy bars. Alvin, Pete and Elmer gave us some."

"Have you got any on you?" asks Bert, but before Bob can say that we ate them, we hear voices across the road. We are in luck! These are American voices and they are coming towards us.

"You ask, Dot," Bert hisses. "They like girls. Remember, say 'Got any gum, chum?'" He pushes me forward.

"Um, hello, sir," I squeak, my voice just making it.

There is quite a group of them and we are pushed backwards as they come to a halt in front of the chemist's shop.

"Hello there, little miss. What can we do for you, down there?" says a voice a long way up.

"Um, can we sing a song for you?"

Mike comes forward. "We sing at the Chapel, sir, and we could sing any hymn or song you want."

"Did you hear that?" says the man, turning to his friends. "What a great offer! Guys, we would love to hear you sing. How about 'There'll Always Be an England'?"

There is a kerfuffle as the men arrange themselves around us. I can't see Elmer, Alvin or Pete but it is dark and they are so tall, maybe they are there somewhere.

We sing the Vera Lynn song. I've heard it on the wireless countless times and know most of the words. When we stop, one of the men shouts, "Encore!", which Jack thinks means sing another one. This time we push Mike forward and he opens his mouth to sing "Once in Royal David's City" and the voice that comes out sounds like heaven and angels and sunshine all at the same time. When he has finished there is a sort of silence and no one moves and one of the men sounds like he is crying.

"Gee," says one of them eventually, "that sure was the best early Christmas carol I've ever been given. What about you fellas?"

The others all agree. They whoop and clap and we stand and wait. Mike's voice is something grown-ups love. I hope the Americans love it enough to give us candy.

Sure enough, the tall man bends his knees and comes right down to our level.

"Now let's see. How would you little troopers like some candy and gum? Shall I give it to the beautiful little girl here?"

I cup my hands together and they pour in candy and gum. We thank them and they thank us and then they head on to the pub. "See you at the boogie-woogie," says one of them. "We might just get you up to sing," he adds, and waves a cheery goodnight.

"What's a boogie-woogie?" asks Bert, but no one knows.

Jack suggests we go over to the Old Mill to share out the candy. As we get to the bottom of Top Road, a raucous yell fills the air, followed by a loud squeal. Bob grabs my hand. Before we have time to move, the cry

101

comes again and then I hear Grandfather Compton's voice coming from the muddy patch in front of the Old Mill. Jack motions us to follow him. We creep along behind him, Bert bringing up the rear.

"Why did you let it go, Arthur?" Grandfather Compton is saying in a cross voice.

"I didn't let it go," says Uncle Arthur. "It was wet and slippery, and it just slid out of my arms."

"How are we going to find the bloody thing in this light," barks Grandfather Compton, "never mind catch it."

Several shadowy figures are running around and while we don't have to be afraid as we know who is here, I wonder what they are doing. Bob drops my hand.

"What are you doing, Grandfather? Can I play?"

To my utter surprise, it is Father who turns around to look at him, his face dark under his pit cap.

"Is that you, Bob? What are you doing here? Are Jack and Dot with you?"

Before I can reply, Uncle Arthur staggers backwards, a long loud squeal fills the air, and as his legs fly up from under him Uncle Arthur lands with a resounding thud at Grandfather's feet.

"It's a piggy. It's a piggy!" laughs Bob. "It's over there. Look!"

Bob's eyes are sharper than anyone else's as we all seem to find it hard to make out much in the darkness and by the time we reach where Bob has pointed, there is nothing there.

"I can't see a bloody thing," complains Mr Walker, one of Father's friends who lives across the road from us. "Where is that ruddy swine?"

Father takes the group of us aside. There are now six wide-eyed children looking up at him.

"Hmm!" he says as he rubs his hand across his face. "You see, this pig got away. And now it has run off into the broken stones by the Old Mill and we can't get it. We can't see it in the dark."

There are so many questions I want to ask, beginning with why the pig was out of its pen in the middle of the night, but something tells me this is the no good Mother was complaining about earlier, so I keep quiet.

"And seeing as you are all here . . ." Father looks across at us. "You might be able to help us if it gets into a small place where we can't reach it."

"We need some light," says Uncle Arthur.

"I've got my bike lamp, if that will do," says Mr Walker.

"All right, all right. But steady now. We don't want the whole bloody village in on this." Grandfather sounds agitated. He points to a pile of rocks. "Shine your lamp there, lad. Bob, get down as far as you can and see what you can see."

Bob is pushed to the front and there is a lot of shushing. With heads down and bottoms up, we all peer into the crack between the rocks, from which there now shines a pair of beady eyes.

"It's in there!" Bob squeals.

"What is?" comes a voice behind us.

"The piggy, the pi —" A hand goes over Bob's mouth.

There is silence. The lamp is switched off and as one we all rise and turn to face the questioner. Constable White! For once he has shown up in time for the action.

"A *pig*?" he repeats, the question hanging in the air.

He turns his bicycle lamp to face us. Father pulls us behind him with his arm across us. Grandfather comes to attention first.

"Ah. Good evening, James," says Grandfather. "Didn't see you there."

The constable does not reply, but tries to look past our group into the rocks.

"A pig? There? Here?" he asks, confusing himself.

There is silence, a shuffling of feet. I can feel Father square up.

"Umm!" says Father. "Yes. A pig, James. It's just the runt of the litter. Don't think it will make much. Hardly worth marketing, so we decided to move it."

Constable White looks around him. "There are rather a lot of you here to move one runt of the litter, Joe. Or were you moving it to some place safe, like your, er, old slaughterhouse, Mr Compton?"

Before he shut up his slaughterhouse, everyone knew Grandfather as the man who sold his own meat.

Constable White straightens the strap of his helmet, the light from his lamp lighting up Grandfather's face. He walks a few paces sideways. In silence Grandfather follows.

While they are talking, Mike whispers that we have to share out the candy and gum. We huddle in a group and I give the goodies to Jack. We each have one candy bar and two sticks of gum. There is one candy bar over and I say that Mike should have it. Bert starts to object but Jack says he thinks that's fair enough.

I put my share in my pocket. Jack and I will get Bob's gum off him later. He is too little to eat it and we will tell him it's too dangerous in case he swallows it and it glues his insides together.

Grandfather is still talking to Constable White, waving his hand towards where the pig is hiding. At first they seem to be arguing, but a few moments later Constable White throws his leg across his bike, his cape over his shoulder, and is gone.

"Right-o. That's him sorted," says Grandfather, clapping his hand on Jack's shoulder. "Now then, how do we get that pig out from those rocks?"

As we peer down the gap in the rocks, a group of miners returning from work stop to see what has been going on.

"All right, Joe. What's going on here?" says one of them.

Father beckons for them to come nearer. They are so blackened with coal dust, it is almost impossible to see them; the whites of their eyes and the yellow of their teeth are the only features I can make out. He asks them if they can help move the rocks, and says that there will be "something in it" for them if they stop.

"Make less noise about it! Hurry up and get that pig out," Grandfather calls in a loud whisper.

In the light of one bicycle lamp, the men begin to throw the rocks sideways.

"Careful you don't hit someone," says Father. "Children! Get back."

We have now been joined by a couple of lads from down Crich Lane. The crowd is growing. Jack, Mike, Bert and Arthur are not pleased to see them, telling them to stand well back as there is a dangerous animal at large.

"What they doing?" one of them asks, as rocks roll down the heap.

A rock hits one of the miners and he falls forward at the exact moment the pig makes a break for freedom. His landing is softened by the pig. I see what happens first.

"Hang on to it!" I yell. "Hang on!"

Father has removed his coat and now he throws it over the pig's head. There is a flurry of bodies and coats, and in a roar of men's voices and pig squealing, all comes to a standstill.

"Run for it!" shouts Grandfather.

I grab Bob's hand and chase after Father, who has the pig in his arms underneath his coat.

In a long line everyone else follows down the gitty. What started as my grandfather, my uncle, my father and Mr Walker chasing a pig has turned into a long convoy made up of miners on their way home, people who live on the gitty and a good many children.

Father shouts over his shoulder, "You three, get in the house. Bert, Arthur, Mike, off home now. Thanks for your help, lads."

When we get home, Mother opens the door. Although a lovely smell of cooking follows her, her face looks hard and stern.

"In!" she commands. Bob starts to tell her what has happened. Mother silences him.

"Take your hats and gloves off and leave those muddy shoes in the kitchen."

"But I want to go to the lavatory," Bob moans.

Mumbling something about this wayward family of hers and she hopes Mrs Walker isn't in there "doing her business", she pulls on her shoes and opens the door to the garden. Light shines over the wall that separates our gardens from the old slaughterhouse yard. We can hear people talking and laughing and from the dancing shadows that leap over the wall, it seems there is quite a lot of activity going on over there. What started as a secret has become a bit of a village affair.

"Can we go and look?" I ask in a small voice.

Mother does not even answer. With her hand behind Bob's head and the candle in the other hand, she marches down the path without a sideways glance. We follow in silence.

As we come back up the path, the gate bursts open. I see Father's smiling face. There is blood on his hands.

"Nellie, we've done it! There'll be pork chops for dinner. There's no problem. We've paid Constable White off with his Christmas dinner, and half the village is in there."

"Joe," says Mother in her very sternest not-to-be-argued-with voice, "I don't care who is there. If any of that meat crosses that doorway, I will leave by the other door. Now get inside you children and I don't want to hear another word about what happened."

"Piggy-wiggy, boogie-woogie," whispers Bob, happy to have been part of this adventurous night.

★ ★ ★

In the end we eat the pork chops round at Grandma Compton's after Chapel on Sunday. I can't remember what it is like not to be hungry for most of the day, but after this meal I think I will be full-up for ever. When we come home, Mother is in a rare good mood.

"Have you seen what's happening tonight at the village hall, any of you?" she asks. None of us have. "A boogie-woogie and jive concert put on for us by the Americans. Imagine that! Dancing! Here in Rompton!" She looks happy and bright.

Father does not look so keen. "Tonight?" he asks. "Wild music on our day of rest?"

"It's not my day of rest, Joe," says Mother, "and I'm going. You lot can come with me or not. Time we had a bit of cheer in this place."

And so it is that at seven o'clock we squeeze into the already packed hall. The last time I was in here an ARP warden had given us a dusty warning about not forgetting our gas masks when we went out. But tonight the little old stage has been transformed: gone are the old curtains, the wood surrounding it has been painted white, and it is flooded with bright light. Golden stripes cover the back curtain, making it glimmer and shine like fairyland. The piano is clean and polished and there are some drums next to it. The place is hopping. My aunts and uncles, our neighbours and friends, the whole village it seems, have come to hear the boogie-woogie.

And then the Americans come on stage, their smart army uniforms gleaming. I recognise the man who gave us candy. And there is Pete, who we taught to play

108

cricket in our garden, and as he sits down at the piano, he spots me at the front and gives me a wink. I feel myself go red. Two soldiers carry out large shiny instruments that they hold up and put to their lips and as the drums roll, the music starts. Pete's fingers fly across the piano, making the most exciting sound I have ever heard. It's choppy, fast, rolling, powerful, and I start jumping up and down, dancing like I will never stop. "Good evening, ladies and gentleman, thank you for having us here in your mighty fine village. We are the Glen Miller Lookalikes and we are here to entertain you . . ." says a soldier who has come out to sing. "Now let's *jive*!"

I look around the hall. Some of the American soldiers have arrived and are swinging our ladies round to the music. The place is jumping with life and there is so much laughter and movement in the room, it feels as if the jive could light up the night sky. It makes me have a thought outside myself: I haven't seen all the people of our village enjoying themselves for so long. It feels magical and I want it to go on for ever.

And suddenly, there among the whirling skirts is Mother. She has taken to the beat and is spinning around with Alvin. She looks happier than I have ever seen her, like all the troubles she carries around with her have flown away. I watch her for a bit and then go to find Father so that he can jive with me. He is standing by the door with some of his workmates from the mine, clutching a bottle of beer like he never wants to let it go.

"Come and see — Mother is jiving! I want to jive too!" I shout.

"I've seen her," he replies. "She'll have a backache and a headache tomorrow. But let her enjoy her dancing while she can. Go and join her, Dot. I can't dance like that. I need to sort out Ernie here."

The ARP man has arrived and does not look best pleased. "If you think you can get this lot out of here and the blackouts down, you are a better man than me," Father tells him. He hands him a beer.

"Maybe you're right, Joe," he says. "If the siren goes off tonight no one will hear it anyway. And I do like a good dance." And with that he heads into the hut, taking off his metal helmet and tucking it under his arm. I pull Father as hard as I can and he comes in and we do a dance that isn't really a jive but is good enough for me. Jack is jiving with June and he must take after Mother as he's pretty good at it.

When the music ends, the cheering must be heard as far as Germany. The man who gave us the sweets asks if the "young man with the beautiful voice and his friends" are here, and as we go forward, the room erupts once again. "Come up here," says the piano man, "and let's close the evening with 'God Save the King'."

Mother's mouth falls open as all three of her children step on to the stage. She is sweaty and shining and happy. I smile at her as we start off the National Anthem and she salutes me back. Boogie-woogie magic.

CHAPTER
SEVEN

All is gathered in

June–October 1944

The Americans leave our village to go to France to help all the people on our side who are fighting the Germans. Alvin, Pete and Elmer come to say goodbye and we have tea and Mother starts to cry. When Alvin tells her she is the best jiver this side of the pond, she laughs through her tears. Alvin says he will always remember us for the kindness we showed him. "If you ever find yourself in our neck of the woods," he says, "there will always be a place for you to stay."

A few weeks later, as the pale sun is coming through to warm us up a bit, Father comes home shouting to Mother to turn on the wireless. He says we need to be absolutely silent and to listen hard because we are about to hear some very good news. The newsreader's voice is as calm as ever, but what he tells us makes me go cold and prickly, in a good way. And though I can't understand all he is saying, I do understand that because all the Allies have worked together in France, the Germans have lost a lot of their soldiers.

We hear shouting from outside our house. Jack is sent to investigate and comes back to tell us that everyone is out in the streets, dancing and cheering. Father turns off the wireless.

"Come on, then!" he says happily. "Let's go and see what's to do. This might mean the war is finally over."

But as we come to see, even though the D-Day landings mean that the Germans are weaker, I don't think it's over because Mrs Baker gets a telegram to say that Mr Baker has died and Bert and Arthur don't have a father any more. I feel very, very bad for singing and dancing in the streets. The man from the Co-op and Grandma Compton's sister's son, Uncle George, also lose their lives and I am too frightened to ask what has happened to Alvin and Elmer and Pete.

We know for sure that the war isn't over yet because one morning Mrs Meeks gathers the whole school together to tell us that because our capital city continues to be targeted by the Germans, we are going to have to help look after some children from London — evacuees — who need to live in a safer place until the V1 bombs stop coming.

Mother tells us that we can't take any children because we haven't got any room but they arrive and get distributed around the village. There is a scramble in the village to get them some warm clothes, even though it is mild outside. "It must be a different climate in London," says Aunt Lily when she comes round to see if we have any spare woollen clothes. We are astonished that she has agreed to take a little girl of my age called Rose, who so far has refused to come out of the bedroom. She has wet the bed so many times that Aunt Lily has asked Mother for Bob's rubber sheet.

Aunt Lily asks me to help. I stand outside Rose's door and tell her very softly that I am called Dot, that Aunt Lily is my aunt, that I live next door but one, that I don't have any sisters, that I would love to play with her and that she and I can be friends.

The door opens slightly.

"Shall I come in?" I ask. No answer comes but I feel brave.

A very thin girl sits cross-legged on the bed. Her face is pale and light brown hair hangs down to her shoulders. She is wearing one of Aunt Lily's cardigans and looks shrunken and small and very, very sad.

Rose just looks at me and doesn't speak, but she pats the bed and I jump up and sit cross-legged opposite her. "Thank you, Dot," she says, in such a small voice I can hardly hear her. Her eyes sparkle with tears. Her hand reaches for mine and I take it and hold it and after a few minutes I ask her where she is from.

"Beffnal Green," she says. "Our 'ouse was bashed by the bomb and me dad was on the docks in Silvertown and it got bombed and no one has found 'im and I miss 'im and I'm scared so far away from me mam." At this, tears slide down her cheeks and she starts to cry properly. But she has spoken and this gives me hope.

"You can share my father," I say kindly. "My dad's a miner and very nice. Do you want to come to my house and meet him?"

She nods and together we go downstairs and I take her out the back door, across the garden paths and to my house. She holds my hand very tight but she has stopped crying and something about her trust in me makes me know for certain that we are going to be friends. We go into the houseplace and without me even saying a word, Father gets up and welcomes her to our house. He tells her that he hopes she will feel very comfortable coming and going between ours and Aunt Lily's house and that this is to be her Derbyshire home for as long as needs be "and beyond". And then Mother bustles in with some jam tarts on a plate and she invites Rose to sit down and she asks her all about the East End of London and before too long Rose is talking and talking and talking and I look at my mother and my father and feel like the luckiest girl alive.

Rose and I become firm friends. But she is fragile and doesn't like to be out of the reach of an adult, so I tell the gang she won't want to come to the first proper meeting between the evacuees and our gang. Jack and his friends have asked Harold, the oldest evacuee, if he wants to get a group together and meet us in the Old Mill ruins. About ten of them turn up and Harry points to show them where we can play war battles.

"Call that a ruin?" smirks Harold. "We got thousands bigger than them in London. Brand-new, smoking piles of rubble. Just been 'it by them V1s."

"Yeah, Harold," says a girl wearing a bright red cap, "this is rubbish. Don't say yes."

"How about a game of tick in the Mill Fields then?" suggests Jack.

"Can't play on them Mill Fields," says Bert, trying to sound like a Londoner. "They put a notice up. They're growin' 'tatoes."

"We could play on those," I say, pointing to the large oak trees that grow along the edge of the field. Their thick gnarled branches and lovely canopy of leaves, bright and glowing in this light, give us endless pleasure. We climb them all year, scrambling up and down, jumping down from the branches to frighten each other.

Two of our visitors stand beneath one of the monster trees and look up at its branches.

"How do you play with a *tree*?" asks the girl.

"Don't know what they're talking about," says their leader. "It's bleedin' cold here. Play on your trees if you like, country bumpkins. We're off."

The evacuees gather up behind him and start to walk back. "Tell you what," Harold calls over his shoulder, "we'll meet you here after tea and teach you some proper games. Bring matches."

We tell Mother that we have to meet the evacuees after tea. She doesn't mind. She has got a new glow about her since the evacuees arrived, helping at the village hall when they were shared out. She told us they all had labels around their necks and that she knew how they felt, "poor, confused, forlorn little mites, so far from home". She hurries us out after we have finished

115

eating, telling us only to remember to "make them feel welcome".

The light is soft and lovely and the sun still buttery, but I am not altogether sure of what is to come. Arthur and Bert aren't allowed to come, but Jack, Harry, George, Mike and I are there to meet them: Harold, the girl with the red cap who tells us she is called Annie, and two more boys: Stan, who has no front teeth, and John, who has an uneven fringe that goes in a diagonal across his forehead.

"Come on then. We'll show you what you do." Harold leads the way back to the road, Annie following and the other two looking at us and laughing. Harry glances back at us and then, nodding his head towards them, sets off with a swagger. Mike and George catch up with him; Jack looks over his shoulder at me and beckons for me to come. I stay firmly at the back.

We walk up Top Road and stop in front of a row of houses.

"Right. This is what you do," announces Harold, the other three standing behind him like soldiers on parade. "You go over and knock on one of those doors, and then you run."

"What for?" asks Mike.

"Blimey. Don't you know nothing?" sneers Harold. "When they answer the door and nobody is there, they'll come out and look up and down the road. It's a laugh. Knock, knock, Ginger."

I stand and look at him, unsure whether I have heard, or understood, what he's said.

"When you've done it for the third time, they get real mad and do some daft things," Harold continues.

I look at the door before which we have stopped. I know that the man who lives here hurt his leg at the pit and can't work. Father has been to see him to tell him he can rest until his leg is better. I tell the boys.

"Then he'll do dafter things," says Harold. "You go first!"

Harry tells me to do what Harold says. I don't want everyone to think I am a sissie, so I go up to the front door and knock on it and run away as fast as I can. We crouch down and watch as the man answers the door, looking up and down to see who's there. He shakes his head and shuts the door.

"Again!" hisses Harold.

But this time, I just can't run away and so I wait until he answers the door.

"Aye, lass?" he says when he sees me standing there. "What can I do for you? Are you all right?"

I am so flummoxed that I tell him my father hopes his leg is better. He thanks me and closes the door.

Next it is Harold's turn. He knocks on a door and runs away and does it three times, the woman in the house getting crosser each time. When he comes back, Mike tells us all to lie low. He has spotted Ernie, the ARP man, doing his rounds.

We watch as he knocks on the doors opposite us. When he gets to the woman we have knocked up three times, we hear her window slide open.

"Whoever you are," she yells, emptying a bucket of water over Ernie's head, "take *that*!"

"Run!" shouts Harold, and we run, like we've never run before. Harry leads the way down a narrow alleyway and when he thinks we are safe he stops. And then we collapse with laughter.

And from that moment, we are friends. For the next few weeks, we see them as much as we can in and after school. And while Rose remains quiet and never wants to come out and play with the others, she and I see each other every day. She is brilliant at drawing and has a set of pencils that she shares with me. While we sit at Aunt Lily's houseplace making pictures, we talk and talk and talk and I ask Mother if Aunt Lily, who doesn't have her own children, could keep Rose for ever.

When we hear on the wireless that the place in Germany that makes the V1 bombs has been hit and Father says he thinks it will be safe for Rose and the other evacuees to go back home, I am sad. Mother hears me crying when I am in bed and comes up to talk to me.

"Think of Rose's mother," she says gently. "I couldn't bear to be parted from you, Dot, for even a night, so imagine what she has been going through. And Rose misses her mother, especially with her father missing for so long. So, it's best for everyone that she goes home."

Rose and I promise to send each other pictures. We hug each other very tight. I cry when she leaves but think of her mother waiting to see her in London. Aunt Lily seems even sadder than me. She has become softer and kinder, and I have enjoyed spending time with her round her table. Rose has her mother, my mother has me, I have Rose as a friend, but Aunt Lily has no one and so I make a promise to myself that I shall go round to her house more so that she isn't sad and lonely.

After the evacuees go, our lives are a bit empty. But there is a lot to do as harvest time is approaching. Father, Jack, Bob and I are busy at the Convict Gardens, working the allotments, to do our bit for England. We are, according to Father, "reaping the fruits of our labour". All must be gathered in so Mother can store food for the coming winter. As we wheel our barrow down Crich Lane, Father tells us we'll be clearing the broad beans today. Passing Starve-to-Death Field, we wait for Father to repeat the story of the men who, more than twenty years ago, queued down the lane here to see if they could get a job as a ganger on the railways or down the mine. "If they didn't get a job, they knew their families would starve to death." And then we cross over into the allotments, Father waving hello to his friends, who are all out tending their plots.

The broad bean plants are very high and my arms start to hurt. Leaving Jack to carry on at the allotment, Father, Bob and me take a break and walk further down the lane where last week we gathered hazelnuts, to see if we can find some rose hips. Spotting a bush that is still full, Father puts his handkerchief around the long branch and lifts it up so we can see the bright red hips. Bob and I pick as many as we can before the branch slips out of Father's grasp. I get a great big thorn in my hand and yell as Father presses his strong thumbs to pop it out. Last year Mother took the rose hips to the clinic and swapped them for cod liver oil and malt. There are posters around the village that show rose hips are full of Vitamin C, and as we can't get oranges to make orange juice any more, we have plenty of roses and their hips can keep us healthy. We walk further up to find a big horse chestnut, its red and brown oval leaves heavy with nuts, the spiky cases bursting open. Sweet chestnuts are a treat at Christmas, roasted over the fire on the ash pan, and we help Father pick them. Mother loves chestnuts and we even manage to find some beech nuts, which Father says he will put away as a surprise for her when she is feeling tired from all the work she does for us.

On the way home — a trudge when we are this exhausted — Father says we can see if the ice-cream sign is still hanging. But as soon as we reach the top of Crich Lane, a high-pitched screech fills the air. I have never heard this noise before and we all stop and look up. Red flames are shooting through the sky, like the flame on the gas, and it looks fiery and hot and dangerous. "It's a buzz bomb!" screams Jack. "And its flame has just gone out! Run!"

"Go up to the Mill Pond!" shouts Father. "I'll go home for your mother."

We run as fast as we can, villagers streaming out of their homes, making for the Mill Pond. The posters in the village tell us to be out of our houses in a shelter or an open space if a bomb falls.

"Has it landed?" someone shouts.

"It's on its way to Sheffield to bomb the steelworks, I reckon," says Mr Burton.

"Why didn't they sound the siren?" asks Mrs Broome.

"I don't think they know where they are going," replies Mr Walker. "I thought we were beating the buggers now. Daren't come over and face us, have to send bombs on wings."

An elderly lady who lives in the big house behind the wall by the Old Mill faints, and ladies with their hands to their faces are crying. For the moment, the bomb is forgotten as people gather to comfort each other. Finally the monster passes over us, its flames burning. The ARP wardens tell us we can go home.

The ice cream is forgotten and we walk home, frightened, tired and fed up. At least Father managed to get the wheelbarrow home, and in the evening, as a treat, he takes out the beech nuts and we eat them around the table as we play a game of cards and Mother listens to her Saturday-night music on the wireless.

As the summer draws to an end and the leaves start to fall and turn, I am commissioned by Aunt Lily to help her with the Harvest Festival. Jack and I walk over to the Chapel with the bundles of corn we have gathered from Uncle George's farm and I am amazed at the glorious colours that greet me; such an array of autumn flowers that she has gathered. There is also a bowl of red, green-gold apples and as always these days, my tummy rumbles and I start to dream about food. My favourite meal of this time — freshly picked peas, new potatoes and mint sauce — is never far from my mind. Neither are onions and potatoes, boiled together with salt, pepper and vinegar. I wonder what the German children are eating. Even though they are my enemy, I wouldn't want them to go hungry too.

At home, the wicker Bo-peep basket with its wide top and long handle stands on the table in the houseplace. It is dusty from being in the cupboard all year. When I get back from the Chapel I help Mother clear the cupboard out so that she can stock it with her autumn preserves. Beautiful strawberry jam, blackcurrant jam, bottled tomatoes, and apple puree all rest quietly, waiting the foodless, cold winter days. We put Grandfather's red apples in the bottom of our clothes drawers. Father always moans that his shirts and underwear smell like a bottle of cider at this time of year.

"So what are we having in the basket?" asks Jack.

"I've left a nice-sized turnip and three good-sized white potatoes on the shelf in the hen house," replies Father. "They should fill the bottom of the basket." The sack of potatoes that rests in the hen house during the winter months stands just inside the door and Father's precious onions hang over it in several bunches, their green stalks tied.

We start to fill the basket. The turnip is exactly the right size for the bottom and the white potatoes fit around it as though that is where they were grown to be. We add some of the red apples and then Mother,

Bob and me set off on our pilgrimage to one of my favourite places in the village.

Grandfather is waiting for us. He lifts a key, which hangs on a string, from his waistcoat pocket, and pushing it into a rusty keyhole in the lower wooden part of a glass and wooden door, he lets us into his greenhouse. "Come on in," he says, "and shut the door before the place goes cold."

Grandfather's tomato plants stand over me. They are tall and majestic and their branches are bowed with fruit, bright red to green. But the most wonderful thing about this place is the warm soft feel and smell that is always there, even on a cold winter's day. The warmth comes from coal that he puts onto a fire, which burns behind a metal door outside on the back wall so that warm water passes through pipes under the benches. The air, perfumed with the smell of the plants, also has the sweet tang of horse manure mingled with it.

Grandfather's most famous and most precious plant is a grape vine that starts its life outside the green-house, its roots buried in earth in a large metal tub. It grows in through a gap at the top of the back wall of the greenhouse and in the spring its branches, which Grandfather attends non-stop, grow along the roof. In late spring there are little green grapes, but now in the autumn, as Grandfather reaches up and parts the browning leaves, bunches of dark-red velvet fruits appear. I have seen the grapes on previous years but they always take my breath away, they are so beautiful, in colour and in grace.

123

"Well, will these do then?" Grandfather's voice makes me jump.

"Oh, they are lovely," says Bob.

"Don't touch them, Bob, or you will ruin the bloom. Let me get them down and tie them on."

Every year, or for as many years as I can remember, our basket has been presented at the Harvest Festival with one of Grandfather's bunches of grapes hanging from its handle and over its contents. As grapes are a fruit that we have never seen for sale in the village, our basket, with its display of this precious fruit, is the star attraction. Before the fruits make it to the table, in front of the Chapel altar, many fingers have sneaked a little touch.

On the day of Harvest Festival we carry our baskets and boxes into Chapel, piled high with prized vegetables and fruits. Soon the table and the carpeted area by the altar rail is covered with offerings.

"So many gifts to God, I see." Mr Compton seems overcome by the wonderful array. The Chapel is full and I sit with June on the front row of the pews. We sing "We plough the fields and scatter the good seed on the land", and then Mr Compton stands before the pulpit and thanks the Lord for giving us so much.

"But above all," he continues, "we should thank God for allowing us to drive all those who would invade us from our shores. And we ask Him for His mercy for those who gave the ultimate, their lives."

Voices call amen and with head bowed I think of Arthur and Bert and Mrs Baker and Uncle George. I also pray for Uncle Jim, who is sailing in what Father calls "dangerous waters". And now I press my hands together even harder and pray that Aunt Flo will return home safe.

Mike sings "The Lord Is My Shepherd" and Mrs Baker has to leave the Chapel. As we all join together to sing hymn number 124, the sheaves of corn tied to the top altar rail start sliding towards the altar. The organist sounds a great peel of chords, and as if to prove that they have all been gathered in, the heads of corn rise and in a golden and brown shower they tumble and turn and Mr Compton, in full voice, disappears beneath them. For a moment voices continue to sing and the organist plays, and then the singing fades, and a sound, which we have heard little of late, starts to rise. Just a few shouts of laughter at first, and then, as if in release from all the tension in which we now live, everyone starts laughing.

Aunt Lily rushes over to help Mr Compton to find his way out of stalks of corn. I duck under the altar rail and move some of the baskets of fruit.

Mr Compton is released and the corn heads now lie under the seat of the organ. "Well," says Mr Compton, who still has an ear of corn sticking out of his hair, "the Lord reminded us that we only did the reaping, He grew the corn. But thank goodness it was the reaper he sent to remind us, and not the Grim Reaper."

The food is distributed to those most in need, but in this time of need for us all, some is sold. Mother has two red cabbages, which she pickles. This is Father's favourite and when his tobacco dwindles to nothing and he has to mix it with dry tea leaves to make him think he has more than he's got, Mother puts red cabbage out on the table to help brighten his supper.

Rose sends me a beautiful picture that she has drawn of her and her mother. They are smiling and Rose is such a good artist that I can feel her come off the page, full of life, and I miss her but am happy she is back with her mother. I draw her a picture of our Harvest Festival, making sure to write grapes next to Grandfather Compton's grapes, in case she doesn't know what they are.

CHAPTER
EIGHT

Marshalling my troops

December 1944

I am Field Marshal Dorothy Elizabeth Compton. I have collected the most paper "for the war effort" in our village, so I went from being a General in our School Paper Army to the highest rank in the Country's Paper Army. After I am given my badge at a ceremony in the Odeon cinema, Father salutes me whenever he sees me, though this only lasts for a few days. But on Sunday, at Chapel, I am called before the ladies who are organising the Christmas Bazaar and congratulated on my achievement, especially on getting Mrs James to part with her dead husband's books even though his memory was, for her, still alive in the pages of his favourite stories.

"A most extraordinary success, Dorothy," says Mrs Parker. "And now that we know how persuasive you can be, we would like to appoint you chief toy collector and stallholder for the forthcoming Christmas bazaar."

"You may like to rally your troops," says Mrs Harrison, laughing, though I am not quite sure at what.

Teamwork is what it is all about, according to Father. I ask June if she will help me and as soon as Jack hears that June has said yes, he offers to help too. And as soon as Bert, Arthur, Mike, George and Harry hear that Jack has said he will help because June has offered to help, they all offer to help. I have a squadron of toy collectors and I am in command.

We hold a meeting by our henhouse to discuss tactics. June is allowed to come, the first time she has ever been to my house. I tell her we only have a toilet outside and that we share it with four other houses and advise her to go at her house before she comes. June has a toilet and bathroom inside her house, with a door that closes, and no freezing cold air as you do your business. I don't want her to be uncomfortable at our house.

At first it looks as if we won't be needing to collect anything because all the boys turn up with toys and push each other out of the way so they can be the first to show June. Mike is giving his jigsaw of a Luftwaffe plane sinking into the sea, George and Harry bring some tanks and soldiers, and Bert and Arthur bring their farm set from when they were younger. June doesn't seem all that impressed. We need as many toys as we can get, as soon as we can, so I remind everyone of my rank, tell them to be quiet, divide us into pairs, instruct everyone which roads to go down and drill them to make sure they don't just go to houses with children but visit old ladies as they are the most generous. I instruct them to find wheelbarrows, tell them there is no time like the present and to be off.

128

And obediently — even Harry — off they go. I like being a Field Marshal very much.

June is my partner and we set off to the houses around where she lives. At the first house, the lady knows June and she asks us to come in. But when we tell her why we have come, she says that she can't let any of the toys in the house go because they are "what she has left of her son", who is away fighting in the war. Thinking he must be a lot older than me if he is away for the war, I ask her if he will play with them when he comes back and she stops for a moment and then says she doesn't suppose he will and that he won't miss "a toy or two", and she goes upstairs and comes back down with a bag of marbles and two board games. They go in our wheelbarrow and, triumphant, we trundle on, determined to collect more than the boys.

I get my family to help too. Grandma Compton makes a rag doll out of pieces of old cloth, soft and floppy with bright button eyes; June's father finds a small bike in the attic, polishes it up and repairs the bell; and Father paints an old wooden cart of Bob's, using the remains of his precious tin of green paint. And following our family outing to the military camp last week, Mother says she will pay another visit to see if the German and Italian prisoners of war will donate some of their beautiful hand-made wooden toys — boy dolls with red, blue, green and yellow painted suits, as well as girl dolls in brightly painted dresses; snakes made with parts hinged together; and little trains with coloured wheels. I know these toys will be a success because I am still fascinated by the acrobat my parents bought for me. He whirls and swings on two pieces of string that are stretched between two sticks of wood. When I press the bottom of the sticks together he swings over and over.

Mother has been sad ever since Karl, a German prisoner of war who Father met while he was helping in the Black Boy pub, was moved to another camp. At first Mother was horrified that Father had invited "the enemy" to tea, but Karl was so polite and young, another "poor, confused, forlorn little mite, so far from home", that she invited him over every Sunday. Over the weeks, strange as it seems, we all became friends with him. Karl was the one who found Mother collapsed on the floor when she was ill with coughing a few weeks ago, and he picked her up and wrapped her in the blankets from the beds upstairs and gave her the medicine that made her feel better. When he left, he gave us a ship in a bottle, one of the most beautiful things I have ever seen, and Mother has put it on top of the wireless so we can all be reminded of the enemy. "Men sent to fight us, just the same as the men we have sent over from our village to fight against people like Karl's mother," she says crossly.

On the day of the bazaar, we arrive early to set up our stall. We have a lot of good toys, some of which are new and will make good Christmas presents. The Sunday school room looks very different. Christmas is next week and the wreaths and garlands are hanging across the ceiling and there are bunches of holly around the stalls and a few pine branches dotted about, decorated with red glass Santas. The Christmas feeling stirs in my tummy and I feel excited and nervous all at once. What happens if no one buys our toys?

The room is buzzing with noise and activity and the air feels alive and happy, a bit like in the jiving hut. Table legs scrape and brightly coloured tablecloths float in the air before landing. Instructions are called out from one stall to another. Next to us is Aunt Lily, who is laying out her plants and cuttings, and as I see her open her mouth to tell us what to do, I pull my Field Marshal self out and order the boys to start arranging the toys, small ones at the front, big ones at the back. Astonishingly, they listen and soon our collection of toys is laid across our clothless trestle table. We have already decided how much we will charge for each contribution, so June and I put a note on each one. I save space at the front for the wooden toys. Mother and I decided we shouldn't say that these have come from the prisoners of war. Some people in the village have been uncomfortable that Italian and German enemies have been helping with the potato picking or repairs to the clothes-shop roof, though we have all pretty much got used to the sight of them riding through the village in army lorries, in their grey prison suits. Only Mrs Baker says we should be frightened to go to sleep at night.

We have half an eye on the kitchen, where a procession of sausage rolls, jam tarts and biscuits have been carried. A puff of steam comes from the kitchen door, the big water urn boiling away. No one but Aunt Lily, Mrs Parker and Mrs Harrison are allowed in the kitchen. Even when Bert pretends to need a drink of water, he is made to take it from a hand that appears from inside the kitchen, around a slightly opened door. It's only when Mrs Parker and Mrs Harrison come to inspect our stall that I notice they have crumbs around their mouths.

"Well, Dorothy," says Mrs Parker, "if the country ever needs someone new to organise the troops, you will be the first on the list. Now, here is your float. Once those doors open and our buyers come in, I advise you to keep a clear head and a calm mind. Good luck!"

I panic. What if all the boys from Crich Lane arrive in a mass? What happens if someone comes around the back of our table and takes the money in the float? I put Jack and Harry in charge of guarding the stall and Arthur and George in charge of taking the money. Bert, June and I will serve our customers.

When the door opens at 2p.m. "on the dot", Mr Compton welcomes everyone to the bazaar, though in the stampede even his voice gets drowned out. And then I see what Mrs Parker meant by wishing us luck: we are run off our feet, the wooden toys going down a treat. I see one girl put a colouring book under her jumper, but as some of the pictures are already coloured in, I don't say anything. There is a bit of a fight over June's old bike, but Mrs Parker passes by at just that moment and the argument is settled.

We are about to sell our last few toys when Mrs Harrison comes over and asks if she can "borrow" me.

"We have raffle tickets to sell, Dorothy," she says, "and we think you might be able to shift a few."

She hands me a book of pink tickets and makes me go through a pretend sale. I have to introduce the raffle, the three prizes — "including our first prize, Mrs Hutchings's renowned pink cake", ask them their name, even if I already know it, write it in the ticket next to the spine of the book and then tear the "corresponding" ticket off, hand it to the person and thank them. She makes me do this to Mother, who, having spotted me, is making her way over to where I am standing with Mrs Harrison.

"Now, Dorothy," says Mrs Harrison, handing me the raffle tickets, a pen and the cloth collection bag, "let me see your famous power of persuasion at work." She waves my mother over. "Now, work your magic on your mother. Persuade her to take four tickets for threepence, instead of just one for a penny."

But Mother looks at her firmly.

"Thank you, Mrs Harrison. Just the one please, Dot. We don't have money to burn."

But it seems that other people do. The sight of Mrs Hutchings's splendid pink cake, with Merry Christmas iced on the top — is too tempting to resist, especially this close to Christmas. There is so little to bake with these days, even with the extra festive half-pound of sugar we've all been allowed, that I am rushed off my feet selling the tickets. I have to call Mike, as he is so good at maths and can help me with the money.

Mrs Harrison makes us go round until we have asked everyone, some people more than once, and finally,

133

when she is satisfied, she takes the cloth bag, empties the money from it, shows us how to tear and fold the tickets and put them into the cloth bag. She takes us to the kitchen so we can sit at the small table. There are no cakes, sausage rolls or jam tarts anywhere and the urn has stopped steaming. But as she turns to leave us to our job, she opens a cupboard and from behind a stack of boxes takes down a plate. Mike and I stare in disbelief. There are ten sausage rolls and eight jam tarts and we are frozen in a moment of indescribable joy.

"Can't let our command go hungry, can we? Share this with your troops, Field Marshal Compton! And enjoy!" And with that she salutes and marches out.

Mike and I eat and fold, eat and fold, but we save a tart each for June, Jack, Bert, Arthur, George and Harry. Back at the toy stall and all around us, it seems that everything has been sold. There are still a lot of people about, so when Mr Compton stands on a chair and asks for everyone's attention, it takes a bit of time for the room to quieten. He thanks us all for our generous donations and "fighting spirit" and says the afternoon will conclude with the "grand draw". Before that, however, he lists the Christmas services and tells us that for the first time "since the world went dark, we shall be uncovering the Chapel's stained-glass windows, surely a sign that our Lord means for hostilities to cease". After a chorus of amens, he asks Mr Boroughs to come forward to pick the winning tickets out of the bag. Third prize — a cutting from Grandpa Compton's tomato plants, goes to ticket 43; second prize — two tins of cling peaches, "donated a while back from our

American friends", ticket 67. And first prize — Mrs Hutchings's splendid pink cake, goes to . . . There is a hush . . . ticket 183. A murmur sounds as everyone checks their ticket. And then I see a pink ticket held high and to my great surprise, with head up and shoulders back, I see my mother approaching Mr Boroughs.

Later, Aunt Lily knocks on the door to tell me that our stall raised £6, which is more than it has ever raised before, and that we should be very proud because it means the Chapel committee has more money to share between the Chapel and our village Spitfire Fund for "Charles and any other young men from our village who are lost or missing". She congratulates Mother on winning the cake, adding that she "supposes it will be shared round the family on Boxing Day".

"That woman!" exclaims Mother, as Aunt Lily leaves.

Loud enough for her to hear.

Mother is very busy in the lead-up to Christmas, so sends Bob and me to Rompton market to get the Christmas provisions. Two years ago, when I was much littler, Mother was in hospital with her coughing and I had to go to the market all by myself. In the jostling and worried queue I met a lady, my Christmas Saviour, who helped me get served and I looked for her last year and I look for her this year, but she is nowhere to be seen.

As usual the market is busy and the queues are long, curling round all the stalls that have any kind of food on them. It isn't as cold as usual, only a smither of snow, so we aren't too cold. We have been instructed to get any fruit and vegetables there might be, but Bob and I are more intent on using our coupon for the half-pound of sweets we have been given this Christmas. I tell him to go and choose from the large glass bottles shining with peppermints and aniseed, so that I can do my thing at Ron's stall. Two years ago, he didn't want to serve me, but my Saviour told him what was what and when he heard my mother was in hospital — ". . . dying, Ron. You want this poor little mite to be motherless *and* starving" — he filled my bag and gave me a bit extra.

The women at Ron's stall are in a vicious mood. There is so little food to go round and each of them wants it. "You shouldn't serve children," shouts one woman. "Where's their mam?" But Ron shouts back at them — last year I didn't tell him my mother was alive and well — and takes my coupons. I see him reaching down under his stall and putting two bananas in my bag, more than we could possibly have dreamed of, and I wish him Merry Christmas in a small, sad, but grateful voice and tell him I need to find my "poor little brother".

Just before Christmas Day Matilda, my favourite hen, gets grass stuck in her throat for a third time and Grandfather Compton can't sew her neck up again, so he takes her away, choking and squawking.

"Kill her, if you must, Father," says Mother, her voice hard as nails. "But don't expect me to prepare her for the oven."

And so, on Christmas Eve, Grandma Compton and Aunt Betty bring Matilda home, soft, white and warm, on a plate. I am sitting in the houseplace, the warmth of the fire making me sleepy. I have been drawing another picture for Rose — of our green and red newspaper-painted garlands, our pine-branch Christmas tree decorated with our trusted old fairy, her star wrapped in yet another saved toffee wrapper — and I wonder what sort of Christmas she will be having.

Mother pretends not to see Matilda through the rest of the evening, though what we would have eaten, I don't know, as we have no meat at the ready. I couldn't get any at the market and there was none in the village to be had. On Christmas morning Father pops Matilda into the oven "just to brown her up a bit," and I love her a bit more for providing us with something to eat. But when he brings her to the table, Mother is stony-faced and silent, refusing any meat.

"Nellie," says Father, "she just died. You couldn't keep her alive for ever. What did you want to do? Take this food out into the garden and give it a funeral, or feed your children and keep yourself from getting ill again?"

Without a word Mother stands and lifts across a dish of potatoes mashed with turnips and puts some on her plate. She adds a couple of sprouts and tells us that is "plenty good enough for me, thank you". But when it comes to our Christmas pudding, which, due to a complete lack of currants this year, is a suet pudding filled with Grandfather's summer raspberries, she gives herself a healthy portion and Father relaxes.

"I wonder if Karl has managed to eat," Mother says. "I pray to God that boy is reunited with his mother before next Christmas. I hear they've started fighting again. It's not going to be over this Christmas, that's for sure. How many more 'it'll be over by Christmas'es do we have to hear, Joe?"

And I think to myself that this war has made my mother so sad in her heart, so sad for all the young men fighting each other and all the mothers that have been separated from their children, that I will do all I can to cheer her up, even if it doesn't end soon.

On Boxing Day, as threatened, while the men are in the Black Boy, Aunt Lily, Aunt Betty, Aunt Flo, Grandma Compton, Aunt Doris and Aunt Mabel come in for tea and a slice of pink "Merry Christmas" cake. Jack, Bob and I have looked at that cake in its glass dish so many times, I am surprised it hasn't disappeared with the intensity of our stares.

Squashed on to the settee and around the table, my aunts lean forward as Mother brings the cake in. Aunt Doris, who has come home for Christmas having been cooking for airmen, tells us all about the ways in which she has learned to stretch rations to feed so many and how she has come to see how precious each and every ingredient can be.

After bringing through the teapot and pouring everyone a cup of tea, Mother lifts the carving knife and cuts into the cake. But as she puts it on to the plate, there is a gasp. Grandma and Aunt Doris rise off the settee.

"Oh, Nellie. It's sad!" exclaims Aunt Doris. "That woman didn't leave it in long enough. How did she manage that? What a dreadful waste of ingredients!"

"We can't eat *that*," sneers Aunt Lily. "What a horrible disappointment."

"Still," continues Aunt Doris, "at least we know Nellie didn't bake it. At least you can't accuse her of that, Lily."

Aunt Lily is silenced. Then she gets up and walks out. No one moves for a moment, then Bob says he doesn't mind if the cake is sad, he'll eat it anyway. Grandma Compton says that might give him a tummy ache, and as everyone starts to discuss whether it will or not, Aunt Lily comes back in. She is holding another cake, one that I am sure I spotted being carried into the kitchen at the bazaar.

"A happier cake," she says. "Nellie, could you do the honours?" And with that, the sad cake is forgotten and Aunt Lily says she will have a word with Mrs Hutchings, no longer in our eyes the Queen of Cakes.

Epilogue

December 1945

I am trudging through the snow, my arms laden with shopping from Rompton market. The war might be over but there still isn't that much to eat — though I do have the extra bar of chocolate Ron has saved for me, "to make up for your loss, lass". I am going to give the chocolate to Bert and Arthur, as they are so sad. Their mother still waits for their father to come through the front door, even though we all know he is never coming back. "I haven't seen him dead," she told Mother, "and until I do, I won't believe it."

We celebrated the end of the war with a big party on the village green — a bonfire with baked potatoes, beer for old and young, and dancing all through the day and night. We decorated the village with flags and bunting and for a few days happiness took us over, "our victory" the only thing we could think about.

But then it didn't seem very different — we still had to plant and grow our own food, still use our ration books, Mother still had to do all the washing and housework, Father was still down the pit, and I still had

140

to walk to school in my worn-out shoes. And Bert and Arthur's father was still dead.

There has been some good news though. A man who works for Pears soap came and took a photograph of Bob because of his blond curls; Jack asked June to go to the picture house with him and she said yes; Aunt Doris has become engaged to an airman she met while she was a cook and Mr Brown has come back from the war, a hero for saving the lives of many men. And last week, I got a Christmas card from Rose asking me to come and visit her in London. Father said that if we have the money, I can go with Mother when she next visits her mother and father in Whitechapel.

Now, as I bang open the back door and come in with the shopping, Mother is standing by the kitchen sink, a letter in her hand.

"Dot!" she exclaims. "Put those down and come into the houseplace. Never mind about your wet shoes or coat."

This is a first. I go into the houseplace, where the fire is warm, the Christmas decorations bright. It's two days until Christmas and we have work to do.

"Oh, Dot. Listen to this!" says Mother, her voice wobbling. She takes a deep breath and starts to read:

"Dear Mrs Compton, I am sending you my greetings from Dresden where I am back with my mother. I have told her all about you and how your kindness and the friendship of your family helped me when I was in your country. My mother does not speak English but she has asked me to thank you for helping me when I was so frightened and far from home. She will always have a place for you in our home and I will always have a place for you in my heart. Yours sincerely, Karl Heinz."

Tears are streaming down Mother's face. I run over to hug her and we stay very still for a long time. Not all the fighting in the war has been done on the battlefields or in the skies. Mother has been fighting every day — to feed us, to keep us warm and safe, to protect us. She has battled against pneumonia, she has battled against Aunt Lily's disapproval, she has battled against being so far from her family in London.

"He's alive!" she says finally. "There's a cause for celebration, Dot. Go and put the kettle on and we will write back to him. We can leave the baking until later."

I reach into my pocket. The chocolate — Mother's favourite — is for her. Bert and Arthur won't mind. I am proud to have something to give her.

"And look what I have to celebrate . . ."

Other titles published by Ulverscroft:

AROUND THE VILLAGE GREEN

Dot May Dunn

It's 1939 and little Dot May Dunn is playing with her brothers in their quiet Derbyshire village. The grown-ups' talk of war means little to Dot, but village life is starting to change. When a prisoner of war camp is built close to Dot's village, and a Yankee base is stationed nearby, Dot makes friends with the most unlikely of soldiers. But her friendships are threatened when telegrams start to arrive in the village and the real impact of war bears heavily on this close-knit mining community. Dot's childhood memoir shares the universals of innocence, love, loss and friendships.

BREAD, JAM AND A BORROWED PRAM

Dot May Dunn

It's the end of the 1950s, the war's long shadow is fading. After qualifying as a midwife, Dot has taken a job as a health visitor working from an inner city clinic. Her beat is a maze of streets and alleyways, overflowing with families trying to survive any way they can. Whether at the clinic, visiting cases or retrieving errant parents from pubs, Dot is thrown in at the deep end. As a health visitor, Dot is responsible not just for the babies brought into this world, but an army of toddlers, tykes and tots who all need a helping hand.